THE XXL KETO DIET COOKBOOK FOR BEGINNERS

2000 Days of Delectable Ketosis Meals Using the Metric Measurements and No-Fuss Local Ingredients to Fuel Your Life

Betty J. Lawson

Copyright© 2024 By Betty J. Lawson Rights Reserved

This book is copyright protected. It is only for personal use. You cannot amend, distribute, sell, use, quote or paraphrase any part of the content within this book, without the consent of the author or publisher.

Under no circumstances will any blame or legal responsibility be held against the publisher, or author, for any damages, reparation, or monetary loss due to the information contained within this book, either directly or indirectly.

Limit of Liability/Disclaimer of Warranty:

No book, including this one, can ever replace the diagnostic expertise and medical advice of a physician in providing information about your health. The information contained herein is not intended to replace medical advice. You should consult with your doctor before using the information in this or any health-related book.

The Publisher and the author make no representations or warranties with respect to the accuracy or completeness of the contents of this work and specifically disclaim all warranties, including without limitation warranties of fitness for a particular purpose. No warranty may be created or extended by sales or promotional materials. The advice and strategies contained herein may not be suitable for every situation. This work is sold with the understanding that the Publisher is not engaged in rendering medical, legal, or other professional advice or services. If professional assistance is required, the services of a competent professional person should be sought. Neither the Publisher nor the author shall be liable for damages arising here from. The fact that an individual, organization, or website is referred to in this work as a citation and/or potential source of further information does not mean that the author or the Publisher endorses the information the individual, organization, or website may provide or recommendations they/it may make. Further, readers should be aware that websites listed in this work may have changed or disappeared between when this work was written and when it is read.

Manufactured in the United Kingdom
Interior and Cover Designer: Danielle Rees
Art Producer: Brooke White
Editor: Aaliyah Lyons
Production Editor: Sienna Adams
Production Manager: Sarah Johnson
Photography: Michael Smith

TABLE OF CONTENTS

Introduction	1
Chapter 1: Ketogenic Fundamentals	2
Unveiling High-Fat, Low-Carb Principles	2
Journey into Ketosis	3
Eat & Avoid Guide	5
Chapter 2: 4-Week Meal Plan	7
Week 1	8
Week 2	9
Week 3	10
Week 4	11
Chapter 3: Breakfast	12
Quesadillas with Bacon & Mushrooms	13
Jalapeno & Cheese Waffles with Bacon	13
Low-Carb Egg Muffins	13
Avocado and Kale Eggs	14
Bacon and Cheese Frittata	14
Spicy Egg Muffins with Bacon & Cheese	14
Cauliflower & Cheese Burgers	15
Ham & Egg Broccoli Bake	15
Cheese Stuffed Avocados	15
Italian Sausage Stacks	16
Carrot and Courgette Loaf	16
Mascarpone & Vanilla Breakfast Cups	16
Smoked Ham and Egg Muffins	17
Nutty 'Porridge'	17
Spiced Avocado Egg Boats	17
Tofu Scrambled with Tomatoes & Mushrooms	18
Broccoli & Cheddar Frittata	18
Chocolate Protein Coconut Shake	18
Huevos Rancheros	19
Ricotta Cloud Pancakes with Whipped Cream	19
Lettuce Cups with Mushrooms and Gruyère	19
Asparagus & Goat Cheese Omelet	20

TABLE OF CONTENTS

Turkey and Cheese Egg Bites	20
Spinach Salad with Goat Cheese & Pine Nuts	20
Breakfast Frittata	21
Cheese Ciabatta with Pepperoni	21
Chia Seed and Strawberry Pudding	21
Belgian-Style Waffles with Lemon Cream Cheese	22
Sesame & Poppy Seed Bagels	22
Kale and Broccoli Slaw with Crispy Bacon	22
Chapter 4: Snacks and Appetizers	**23**
Mushroom and Bacon Rolls	24
Garlic and Herb Butter Eggs	24
Dill Pickles with Tuna Mayo	24
Ham and Avocado Devilled Eggs	25
Spicy Glazed Spare Ribs	25
Cheesy Garlic Scones	25
Devilled Eggs with Spicy Mayo	26
Crispy Green Bean and Cheese Straws	26
Strawberry Chocolate Mousse	26
Spicy Chicken and Cucumber Canapés	27
Garlic and Basil Mashed Celeriac	27
Cheesy Cauliflower Gratin	27
Roasted Mixed Nuts	28
Easiest Keto Cheesecake Ever	28
Jalapeno Turkey Tomato Bites	28
Cocoa Nuts Goji Bars	29
Keto Cookie Dough Bars	29
Friday Night Cauliflower Fritters	29
Homemade Cheesy Spinach Balls	30
Easy Salad with Bacon and Avocado	30
Baked Ham & Cheese Egg Cakes	30
Greek Salad with Capers	31
Chocolate Chip Cookies	31
Rum Brownies	31
Cauliflower Salad with Shrimp and Cucumber	32
Stuffed Mini Peppers	32
Two Cheese and Prosciutto Balls	32

TABLE OF CONTENTS

Chocolate Peanut Truffles — 33
Cocktail Meatballs with Cheese — 33
Classic Hot Chicken Drumettes — 33

Chapter 5: Poultry — 34

Buffalo Chicken — 35
Hungarian Chicken — 35
Asian-Style Turkey Soup — 35
Tangy Classic Chicken Drumettes — 36
Easy Turkey Curry — 36
Cheesy Turkey Base Pizza with Bacon — 36
Cheesy Ranch Chicken — 37
Chicken & Squash Traybake — 37
Spicy Cheese Chicken Soup — 37
Spiced Chicken Kebabs with Tahini Sauce — 38
Lemon Chicken Kebabs — 38
Keto Turkey Lettuce Wraps — 38
Roasted Stuffed Chicken with Tomato Basil Sauce — 39
Crispy Cheddar-Coated Chicken — 39
Spicy Chicken Kabobs — 39
Courgetti with Turkey Ragu — 40
Grilled Bok Choy Caesar Salad with Chicken — 40
Creamy Spinach Chicken — 40
Roast Chicken with Brussels Sprouts — 41
Herbed Butter Chicken Legs — 41
Asian-Glazed Chicken Legs — 41
Citrus Beer-Glazed Chicken Wings — 42
Chicken and Spinach Gratin — 42
Baked Buffalo Chicken Wings — 42
Rosemary Chicken with Avocado Sauce — 43
Chicken Puttanesca — 43
Pesto Chicken — 43

Chapter 6: Beef, Lamb and Pork — 44

Classic Homemade Beefburgers — 45
Balsamic Slow-Cooked Beef — 45
Pesto Slow-Cooked Beef — 45
BBQ Pulled Pork Pizza with Goat's Cheese — 46

TABLE OF CONTENTS

Low-Carb Pork Nachos	46
Herbed Pork Chops with Raspberry Sauce	46
Balsamic-Marinated Pork Chops	47
Garlic Steak Bites with Courgetti	47
Paprika Pork Chops	47
Peanut Butter Pork Stir-Fry	48
Courgette Boats with Spiced Beef	48
Sausage, Tomato and Pesto Salad	48
Rich Beef Ragù	49
Warming Winter Beef Ragù	49
Hearty Beef and Spring Onion Soup	49
Traditional Beef Bourguignon	50
Perfect Sunday Roast Beef	50
King-Size Burgers	50
Spiced Beef and Vegetable Soup	51
Stuffed Flank Steak Pinwheels	51
Cauli Rice with Vegetables and Beef Steak	51
Meat and Goat Cheese Stuffed Mushrooms	52
Cauliflower Curry with Minced Beef	52
Bunless Beef Burgers with Sriracha	52
Cheese Beef Burgers with Cauli Rice Casserole	53
Creole Beef Tripe Stew	53
Portobello Mushroom Beef Burgers	53
Chapter 7: Fish and Seafood	**54**
Keto Wraps with Anchovies	55
Haddock Fillets with Mediterranean Sauce	55
Cod with Parsley Pistou	55
Shrimp in Creamy Pesto over Courgetti	56
Salmon with Tarragon-Dijon Sauce	56
Garlic and Chilli Prawns	56
Salt-and-Pepper Scallops and Calamari	57
Mom's Seafood Chowder	57
Lemon and Herb Tilapia	57
Basil Shrimp Stew with Sriracha Sauce	58
Fish Curry Masala	58
Lemon Crab Cakes	58

TABLE OF CONTENTS

Tilapia Cabbage Tortillas with Cauliflower Rice	59
Crispy Salmon with Broccoli & Red Bell Pepper	59
Blackened Fish Tacos with Slaw	59
Chili Cod with Chive Sauce	60
Crab Cakes with Coconut	60
Hand-Rolled Prawn Sushi	60
Baked Trout with Asparagus	61
Traditional Fish Stew	61
Spiced Fish Cakes	61
Mediterranean-Style Tilapia	62
Quick Prawn Jambalaya	62
Cod with Mustard Cream	62
Oriental-Style Fish Stew	63
Steamed Mussels in Coconut Curry	63
Pan-Fried Salmon with Tarragon Mustard Sauce	63
Chapter 8: Vegan and Vegetarian	**64**
Creamed Vegetables	65
Sunday Cauliflower and Ham Gratin	65
Creamy Broccoli and Cauliflower Bake	65
Stuffed Spaghetti Squash	66
Vegetable and Tempeh Kebabs	66
Cheesy Courgette Bites	66
Cauliflower, Cheese and Spring Greens Waffles	67
Broccoli, Mint and Cheddar Soup	67
Courgetti with Avocado and Pesto	67
Cauliflower and Avocado Wraps	68
Courgetti with Avocado and Olives	68
Mushroom Risotto with Cauliflower Rice	68
Roasted Cauliflower Gratin	69
Spanish-Style Stuffed Peppers	69
Avocado and Tomato Wraps	69
Courgette and Spinach Lasagne	70
Spicy Warm Cabbage Salad	70
Creamy Braised Kale	70
Indian-Spiced Cabbage Stir-Fry	71
Cauliflower Gouda Casserole	71

TABLE OF CONTENTS

Broccoli and Cheese Croquettes	71
Chestnut Mushroom Stroganoff	72
Creamy Vegetable Stew	72
Swiss Cheese and Broccoli Bake	72

Chapter 9: Desserts — 73

Five-Seed Crackers	74
Cheddar and Chive Scones	74
Layered Berry and Avocado Fool	74
Frozen Blueberry Pearls	75
Easy Everyday Brownies	75
Slow-Cooker Blueberry Crumble	75
Keto Bread	76
Mini Muffins on the Go	76
Cheesy Cauliflower Fritters	76
Slow-Cooker Lemon Posset	77
Matcha and Macadamia Squares	77
Citrus Mousse with Toasted Almonds	77
Blueberry Tart with Lavender	78
Vanilla Flan with Mint	78
Lemon Cheesecake Mousse	78
Green Tea Brownies with Macadamia Nuts	79
Grandma's Coconut Treats	79
Eggless Strawberry Mousse	79
Coconut Bars	80
Vanilla Pudding with Hazelnuts	80
No-Bake Raw Coconut Balls	80
Keto Fudge	81
Keto Peanut Butter Cookies	81
Peanut Butter Ice Cream	81
Keto Strawberry Ice Cream	82
Old-Fashioned Penuche Bars	82
No Bake Energy Bites	82

Appendix 1: Measurement Conversion Chart — 83

Appendix 2: The Dirty Dozen and Clean Fifteen — 84

Appendix 3: Index — 85

INTRODUCTION

A couple of years back, I found myself in a bit of a rut. I was going to the gym, trying different diets, but nothing seemed to really click. Then, I heard about the keto diet from a friend who was absolutely buzzing with energy and dropping kilos without looking miserable (or hangry, for that matter). I thought, why not give it a go?

The idea of eating fewer carbs was daunting at first. Bread, pasta, and my beloved crisps? Out the window! But I was determined, so I started slow, easing myself into it by swapping sugary snacks for healthier, high-fat options like avocado and nuts. I started experimenting with recipes – who knew cauliflower could turn into such amazing dishes?

The first couple of weeks were honestly a bit of a drag. They call it the "keto flu," but it was more like keto doom. Headaches, feeling tired – my body wasn't happy about this change. But once I pushed through, I woke up one day feeling incredible. I had this clean, lasting energy that seemed to power me through my workouts and my day without crashing.

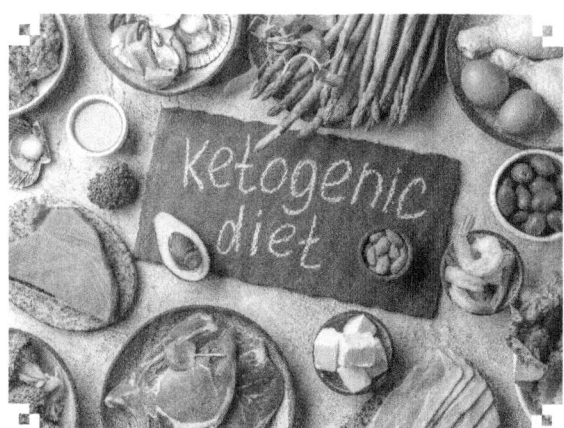

As time went on, keto became less of a diet and more of a lifestyle. My cravings for junk faded, and I grew to love the healthy fats and creative meals I was cooking. The best part? I didn't feel restricted or miserable. I felt... alive, full of energy, and finally at peace with food.

Now, I can't imagine going back. Keto taught me so much about my body and fuel – it's been a game-changer for my fitness and overall wellbeing. Plus, I get to keep eating avocado toast (keto style, of course)!

DEDICATION

Sophia, thank you for introducing me to the world of keto – you've truly changed my life! I never imagined such a lifestyle shift would bring not just health, but so much energy and positivity. You've been my inspiration, guiding me through all the ups and downs of this journey, and it's because of you that I feel so empowered and at peace with food. Beyond that, the experiences and life lessons you've shared have shaped me in ways I'll always treasure. Here's to many more adventures together, and to the amazing gift of friendship you've given me!

CHAPTER 1: KETOGENIC FUNDAMENTALS

UNVEILING HIGH-FAT, LOW-CARB PRINCIPLES

Embarking on the ketogenic journey involves unraveling the core principles that define this dietary approach. At the heart of the ketogenic diet lies a fundamental shift in macronutrient consumption, favoring high-fat and low-carbohydrate intake. Unveiling these principles is not merely an exercise in dietary jargon but a practical exploration of how these choices impact the body and drive it into a state of ketosis.

UNDERSTANDING MACRONUTRIENT RATIOS

In the world of keto, the cornerstone is the manipulation of macronutrients, specifically fats and carbohydrates. Traditional diets often rely on a balanced intake of carbohydrates, proteins, and fats. However, the ketogenic approach flips this script, emphasizing a significant increase in dietary fats while drastically reducing carbohydrate intake. This shift prompts the body to seek alternative energy sources, ultimately leading to the utilization of stored fat for fuel.

THE ROLE OF DIETARY FATS

Contrary to conventional dietary advice, the ketogenic diet champions the consumption of healthy fats. Avocado, olive oil, nuts, and oily fish become not just acceptable but essential elements of daily nutrition. These fats serve as a potent energy source, supplying the body with a sustained and reliable fuel stream. Moreover, they play a crucial role in supporting various bodily functions, including hormone regulation and nutrient absorption.

CARBOHYDRATES: THE NEED FOR RESTRICTION

In the ketogenic world, carbohydrates are not inherently evil, but their consumption is judiciously controlled. The goal is to limit carb intake to a level where the body enters a state of ketosis, characterized by the production of ketones as an alternative fuel source. This typically translates to reducing carb intake to around 5-10% of daily caloric intake, a departure from the standard Western diet.

PRACTICAL IMPLEMENTATION

Translating these principles into practical daily choices is the key to successful keto living. Planning meals that are rich in healthy fats, moderate in protein, and low in carbs becomes a cornerstone of this lifestyle. Opting for leafy greens, non-starchy vegetables, and berries over high-carb options ensures a nutrient-dense approach that aligns with keto goals.

KETOGENIC FUNDAMENTALS

MEAL DIVERSITY AND SATISFACTION

One common misconception about the ketogenic diet is that it lacks diversity and satisfaction. However, with creativity and exploration, a vast array of delicious and filling meals can be crafted within the framework of high-fat, low-carb principles. From avocado and bacon-stuffed omelets to courgette noodles with creamy Alfredo sauce, the possibilities are expansive and exciting.

JOURNEY INTO KETOSIS

Understanding the practical aspects of this journey into ketosis is essential for those seeking not just weight loss but a transformative shift in energy metabolism and overall well-being.

TRANSITIONING FUEL SOURCES

At the heart of the journey into ketosis lies a fundamental shift in the body's primary fuel source. In a typical diet rich in carbohydrates, the body relies on glucose derived from carbs for energy. However, when carb intake is drastically reduced, the body begins to tap into its fat stores, breaking them down into ketones as an alternative fuel. This transition from glucose to ketones is the hallmark of ketosis and a key driver of the ketogenic diet's success.

PRACTICAL ASPECTS OF KETOSIS INITIATION

Initiating ketosis involves more than just slashing carbohydrate intake; it requires a thoughtful and strategic approach. A common starting point is a period of low-carb intake, typically around 20-50 grams per day. This carb restriction signals the body to deplete its glycogen stores, a process that takes a few days and prompts the transition to ketosis.

MANAGING THE KETO FLU

As the body adapts to this new metabolic state, individuals often experience what is colloquially known as the "keto flu." This temporary set of symptoms, including fatigue, headaches, and irritability, is the body's response to the shift in energy sources. Practical strategies, such as staying well-hydrated, increasing electrolyte intake, and gradually reducing carb intake, can help manage these symptoms and ease the transition.

TRACKING MACRONUTRIENTS AND KETONE LEVELS

Practicality in the journey to ketosis extends to monitoring macronutrient intake and ketone levels. Tracking daily carb, protein, and fat intake ensures that the body remains in the desired metabolic state. Additionally, measuring ketone levels, either through urine, blood, or breath testing, provides valuable feedback

CHAPTER 1

on the effectiveness of dietary choices and helps individuals stay on course.

EXERCISE AND KETOSIS

Physical activity plays a crucial role in the journey into ketosis. Exercise not only aids in depleting glycogen stores but also enhances the body's ability to adapt to burning fat for fuel. Implementing a combination of aerobic and resistance training can optimize the metabolic shift and contribute to overall well-being.

SUSTAINABILITY AND LONG-TERM KETOSIS

Beyond the initial transition, the practicality of sustaining ketosis becomes paramount. Incorporating a variety of nutrient-dense, low-carb foods ensures a balanced and enjoyable dietary experience. Experimenting with different recipes and meal plans adds a layer of sustainability, preventing monotony and enhancing adherence to the ketogenic lifestyle.

PERSONALIZATION AND LISTENING TO THE BODY

A practical journey into ketosis acknowledges the individual nature of this metabolic transition. While general guidelines exist, each person's response to the ketogenic diet can vary. Listening to the body, making adjustments based on personal experiences, and consulting with healthcare professionals contribute to a personalized and effective approach to ketosis.

KETOGENIC FUNDAMENTALS

EAT & AVOID GUIDE

KETO FOODS TO ENJOY

HIGH FAT / LOW CARB (BASED ON NET CARBS)

MEATS & SEAFOOD
- Beef (ground beef, steak, etc.)
- Chicken
- Crab
- Crawfish
- Duck
- Fish
- Goose
- Lamb
- Lobster
- Mussels
- Octopus
- Pork (pork chops, bacon, etc.)
- Quail
- Sausage (without fillers)
- Scallops
- Shrimp
- Veal
- Venison

DAIRY
- Blue cheese dressing
- Burrata cheese
- Cottage cheese
- Cream cheese
- Eggs
- Greek yogurt (full-fat)
- Grilling cheese
- Halloumi cheese
- Heavy (whipping) cream
- Homemade whipped cream
- Kefalotyri cheese
- Mozzarella cheese
- Provolone cheese
- Queso blanco
- Ranch dressing
- Ricotta cheese
- Unsweetened almond milk
- Unsweetened coconut milk

VEGETABLES
- Alfalfa sprouts
- Asparagus
- Avocados
- Bell peppers
- Broccoli
- Cabbage
- Carrots (in moderation)
- Cauliflower
- Celery
- Chicory
- Coconut
- Cucumbers
- Garlic (in moderation)
- Green beans
- Herbs
- Jicama
- Lemons
- Limes
- Mushrooms
- Okra
- Olives
- Onions (in moderation)
- Pickles
- Pumpkin
- Radishes
- Salad greens
- Scallions
- Spaghetti squash (in moderation)
- Tomatoes (in moderation)
- Zucchini

NUTS & SEEDS
- Almonds
- Brazil nuts
- Chia seeds
- Flaxseeds
- Hazelnuts
- Macadamia nuts
- Peanuts (in moderation)
- Pecans
- Pine nuts
- Pumpkin seeds
- Sacha inchi seeds
- Sesame seeds
- Walnuts

FRUITS
- Blackberries
- Blueberries
- Cranberries
- Raspberries
- Strawberries

CHAPTER 1

KETO FOODS TO AVOID
LOW FAT / HIGH CARB (BASED ON NET CARBS)

MEATS & MEAT ALTERNATIVES
- Deli meat (some, not all)
- Hot dogs (with fillers)
- Sausage (with fillers)
- Seitan
- Tofu

DAIRY
- Almond milk (sweetened)
- Coconut milk (sweetened)
- Milk
- Soy milk (regular)
- Yogurt (regular)

NUTS & SEEDS
- Cashews
- Chestnuts
- Pistachios

VEGETABLES
- Artichokes
- Beans (all varieties)
- Burdock root
- Butternut squash
- Chickpeas
- Corn
- Edamame
- Eggplant
- Leeks
- Parsnips
- Plantains
- Potatoes
- Sweet potatoes
- Taro root
- Turnips
- Winter squash
- Yams

FRUITS &
- Apples
- Apricots
- Bananas
- Boysenberries
- Cantaloupe
- Cherries
- Currants
- Dates
- Elderberries
- Gooseberries
- Grapes
- Honeydew melon
- Huckleberries
- Kiwifruits
- Mangos
- Oranges
- Peaches
- Peas
- Pineapples
- Plums
- Prunes
- Raisins
- Water chestnuts

KETO COOKING STAPLES

1. Pink Himalayan salt
2. Freshly ground black pepper
3. Ghee (clarified butter, without dairy; buy grass-fed if you can)
4. Olive oil
5. Grass-fed butter

KETO PERISHABLES

1. Eggs (pasture-raised, if you can)
2. Avocados
3. Bacon (uncured)
4. Cream cheese (full-fat; or use a dairy-free alternative)
5. Sour cream (full-fat; or use a dairy-free alternative)
6. Heavy whipping cream or coconut milk (full-fat; I buy the coconut milk in a can)
7. Garlic (fresh or pre-minced in a jar)
8. Cauliflower
9. Meat (grass-fed, if you can)
10. Greens (spinach, kale, or arugula)

CHAPTER 2: 4-WEEK MEAL PLAN

CHAPTER 2

WEEK 1

Day 1:

Breakfast: Sesame & Poppy Seed Bagels

Lunch: Shrimp in Creamy Pesto over Courgetti

Snack: Greek Salad with Capers

Dinner: Cauliflower and Avocado Wraps

Total for the day:

Calories: 1702; Fat: 114.3g; Carbs: 33.9g; Protein: 83.1g

Day 2:

Breakfast: Lettuce Cups with Mushrooms and Gruyère

Lunch: Shrimp in Creamy Pesto over Courgetti

Snack: Rum Brownies

Dinner: Cauliflower and Avocado Wraps

Total for the day:

Calories: 1884; Fat: 146.6g; Carbs: 36.8g; Protein: 81.1g

Day 3:

Breakfast: Sesame & Poppy Seed Bagels

Lunch: Crispy Salmon with Broccoli & Red Bell Pepper

Snack: Greek Salad with Capers

Dinner: Roasted Cauliflower Gratin

Total for the day:

Calories: 1772; Fat: 123.3g; Carbs: 21.8g; Protein: 108.6g

Day 4:

Breakfast: Lettuce Cups with Mushrooms and Gruyère

Lunch: Crispy Salmon with Broccoli & Red Bell Pepper

Snack: Rum Brownies

Dinner: Shrimp in Creamy Pesto over Courgetti

Total for the day:

Calories: 1855; Fat: 144.2g; Carbs: 33g; Protein: 108.9g

Day 5:

Breakfast: Sesame & Poppy Seed Bagels

Lunch: Crispy Salmon with Broccoli & Red Bell Pepper

Snack: Greek Salad with Capers

Dinner: Cauliflower and Avocado Wraps

Total for the day:

Calories: 1774; Fat: 116.3g; Carbs: 24.9g; Protein: 108.1g

Day 6:

Breakfast: Lettuce Cups with Mushrooms and Gruyère

Lunch: Cauliflower and Avocado Wraps

Snack: Rum Brownies

Dinner: Crispy Salmon with Broccoli & Red Bell Pepper

Total for the day:

Calories: 1855; Fat: 144.2g; Carbs: 33g; Protein: 108.9g

Day 7:

Breakfast: Sesame & Poppy Seed Bagels

Lunch: Roasted Cauliflower Gratin

Snack: Greek Salad with Capers

Dinner: Shrimp in Creamy Pesto over Courgetti

Total for the day:

Calories: 1700; Fat: 121.3g; Carbs: 30.8g; Protein: 83.6g

4-WEEK MEAL PLAN

WEEK 2

Day 1:

Breakfast: **Quesadillas with Bacon & Mushrooms**

Lunch: **Hungarian Chicken**

Snack: **Garlic and Herb Butter Eggs (2 Serves)**

Dinner: **Pesto Slow-Cooked Beef**

Total for the day:

Calories: **2011**; Fat: **160.7g**; Carbs: **17.1g**; Protein: **107.6g**

Day 2:

Breakfast: **Cauliflower & Cheese Burgers**

Lunch: **Creamy Spinach Chicken**

Snack: **Easy Salad with Bacon and Avocado (2 Serves)**

Dinner: **Low-Carb Pork Nachos**

Total for the day:

Calories: **2014**; Fat: **162.8g**; Carbs: **26.5g**; Protein: **67g**

Day 3:

Breakfast: **Quesadillas with Bacon & Mushrooms**

Lunch: **Pesto Slow-Cooked Beef**

Snack: **Garlic and Herb Butter Eggs**

Dinner: **Hungarian Chicken**

Total for the day:

Calories: **2010**; Fat: **160.7g**; Carbs: **17.1g**; Protein: **107.6g**

Day 4:

Breakfast: **Cauliflower & Cheese Burgers**

Lunch: **Low-Carb Pork Nachos**

Snack: **Chocolate Peanut Truffles (2 Serves)**

Dinner: **Creamy Spinach Chicken**

Total for the day:

Calories: **1970**; Fat: **162g**; Carbs: **35.1g**; Protein: **66.8g**

Day 5:

Breakfast: **Quesadillas with Bacon & Mushrooms**

Lunch: **Creamy Spinach Chicken**

Snack: **Chocolate Peanut Truffles (2 Serves)**

Dinner: **Pesto Slow-Cooked Beef**

Total for the day:

Calories: **2066**; Fat: **188.9g**; Carbs: **26.1g**; Protein: **90.8g**

Day 6:

Breakfast: **Cauliflower & Cheese Burgers**

Lunch: **Hungarian Chicken**

Snack: **Strawberry Chocolate Mousse**

Dinner: **Pesto Slow-Cooked Beef**

Total for the day:

Calories: **1917**; Fat: **154.4g**; Carbs: **23.4g**; Protein: **81.6g**

Day 7:

Breakfast: **Quesadillas with Bacon & Mushrooms**

Lunch: **Low-Carb Pork Nachos**

Snack: **Strawberry Chocolate Mousse (2 Serves)**

Dinner: **Creamy Spinach Chicken**

Total for the day:

Calories: **2227**; Fat: **183.9g**; Carbs: **35.3g**; Protein: **87.5g**

CHAPTER 2

WEEK 3

Day 1:

Breakfast: **Italian Sausage Stacks**

Lunch: **Lemon Chicken Kebabs**

Snack: **Easiest Keto Cheesecake Ever (2 Serves)**

Dinner: **Balsamic Slow-Cooked Beef**

Total for the day:

Calories: **2026**; Fat: **149g**; Carbs: **24.5g**; Protein: **89.6g**

Day 2:

Breakfast: **Smoked Ham and Egg Muffins**

Lunch: **Lemon Chicken Kebabs**

Snack: **Chocolate Chip Cookies (2 Serves)**

Dinner: **Portobello Mushroom Beef Burgers**

Total for the day:

Calories: **1856**; Fat: **131.5g**; Carbs: **25.5g**; Protein: **98.1g**

Day 3:

Breakfast: **Italian Sausage Stacks**

Lunch: **Balsamic Slow-Cooked Beef**

Snack: **Easiest Keto Cheesecake Ever (2 Serves)**

Dinner: **Stuffed Flank Steak Pinwheels**

Total for the day:

Calories: **2166**; Fat: **179g**; Carbs: **23g**; Protein: **83.6g**

Day 4:

Breakfast: **Smoked Ham and Egg Muffins**

Lunch: **Portobello Mushroom Beef Burgers**

Snack: **Keto Cookie Dough Bars (2 Serves)**

Dinner: **Lemon Chicken Kebabs**

Total for the day:

Calories: **1906**; Fat: **144.2g**; Carbs: **31g**; Protein: **97.6g**

Day 5:

Breakfast: **Italian Sausage Stacks**

Lunch: **Portobello Mushroom Beef Burgers**

Snack: **Easiest Keto Cheesecake Ever**

Dinner: **Balsamic Slow-Cooked Beef**

Total for the day:

Calories: **1770**; Fat: **138.5g**; Carbs: **16.7g**; Protein: **87.8g**

Day 6:

Breakfast: **Smoked Ham and Egg Muffins**

Lunch: **Balsamic Slow-Cooked Beef**

Snack: **Chocolate Chip Cookies (2 Serves)**

Dinner: **Stuffed Flank Steak Pinwheels**

Total for the day:

Calories: **1967**; Fat: **162g**; Carbs: **21.8g**; Protein: **82.1g**

Day 7:

Breakfast: **Smoked Ham and Egg Muffins**

Lunch: **Lemon Chicken Kebabs**

Snack: **Easiest Keto Cheesecake Ever**

Dinner: **Stuffed Flank Steak Pinwheels**

Total for the day:

Calories: **1769**; Fat: **121.2g**; Carbs: **29.5g**; Protein: **101.1g**

4-WEEK MEAL PLAN

WEEK 4

Day 1:

Breakfast: **Bacon and Cheese Frittata**

Lunch: **Cheesy Turkey Base Pizza with Bacon**

Snack: **Roasted Mixed Nuts**

Dinner: **Peanut Butter Pork Stir-Fry**

Total for the day:

Calories:1930.0; Fat:161.9; Carbs:29.5; Protein:88.7

Day 2:

Breakfast: **Jalapeno & Cheese Waffles with Bacon**

Lunch: **Cod with Parsley Pistou**

Snack: **Stuffed Mini Peppers**

Dinner: **Cheesy Turkey Base Pizza with Bacon**

Total for the day:

Calories:1919.0; Fat:155.2; Carbs:22.6; Protein:100.7

Day 3:

Breakfast: **Bacon and Cheese Frittata**

Lunch: **Peanut Butter Pork Stir-Fry**

Snack: **Roasted Mixed Nuts**

Dinner: **Cod with Parsley Pistou**

Total for the day:

Calories:2151.0; Fat:194.2; Carbs:26.6; Protein: 77.1

Day 4:

Breakfast: **Ricotta Cloud Pancakes with Whipped Cream**

Lunch: **Cheesy Turkey Base Pizza with Bacon**

Snack: **Roasted Mixed Nuts**

Dinner: **Courgetti with Avocado and Pesto**

Total for the day:

Calories: 1890; Fat: 157.5g; Carbs: 41.5g; Protein: 69.0g

Day 5:

Breakfast: **Jalapeno & Cheese Waffles with Bacon**

Lunch: **Courgetti with Avocado and Pesto**

Snack: **Roasted Mixed Nuts**

Dinner: **Peanut Butter Pork Stir-Fry**

Total for the day:

Calories: 2465; Fat: 220.5g; Carbs: 36.9g; Protein: 74.8g

Day 6:

Breakfast: **Bacon and Cheese Frittata**

Lunch: **Peanut Butter Pork Stir-Fry**

Snack: **Mushroom and Bacon Rolls (2 Serves)**

Dinner: **Courgetti with Avocado and Pesto**

Total for the day:

Calories: 1991; Fat: 185.4g; Carbs: 20.2g; Protein: 46.8g

Day 7:

Breakfast: **Ricotta Cloud Pancakes with Whipped Cream**

Lunch: **Cod with Parsley Pistou**

Snack: **Mushroom and Bacon Rolls (2 Serves)**

Dinner: **Cheesy Turkey Base Pizza with Bacon**

Total for the day:

Calories: 1994; Fat: 174.7g; Carbs: 24.3g; Protein: 68.1g

CHAPTER 3: BREAKFAST

BREAKFAST

QUESADILLAS WITH BACON & MUSHROOMS

Prep time: **30 minutes** | Cook time: **5 minutes** | Serves **4**

- 500g mushrooms, sliced
- 4 low-carb tortilla wraps
- 4 eggs, hard-boiled and chopped
- 30g butter
- 250g mature cheddar cheese, grated
- 500g Emmental cheese, grated
- 115g streaky bacon
- 1 banana shallot, finely sliced

1. Fry the bacon in a heavy-based frying pan over medium heat for 4 minutes until crispy. Remove, chop and set aside. In the same pan, sauté the shallot and mushrooms in the bacon fat for 5 minutes. Set aside.
2. Melt 15g of butter in a separate frying pan over medium heat. Lay one tortilla wrap in the pan; sprinkle with some Emmental cheese. Add some chopped eggs and bacon over the cheese, top with shallot, mushrooms, and sprinkle with cheddar cheese. Cover with another tortilla wrap.
3. Cook for 45 seconds, then carefully flip the quesadilla, and cook the other side for 45 seconds.
4. Remove to a plate and repeat the cooking process with the remaining tortilla wraps.

Per Serving

Calories: **434** | Fat: **42.7g** | Carbs: **6.1g** | Protein: **27g**

JALAPENO & CHEESE WAFFLES WITH BACON

Prep time: **20 minutes** | Cook time: **10 minutes** | Serves **4**

- 30g butter, melted
- 250ml almond milk
- 4 tbsp ground almonds
- Salt and freshly ground black pepper, to taste
- 5g fresh parsley, chopped
- ½ jalapeño chilli, deseeded and finely chopped
- 4 medium eggs
- 250g mature cheddar cheese, crumbled
- 6 rashers streaky bacon, chopped
- 1 ripe avocado, sliced

1. In a frying pan over medium heat, fry bacon until crispy, about 5 minutes. Remove to a plate lined with kitchen paper. In a mixing bowl, combine the remaining ingredients, except the avocado. Preheat a waffle iron and lightly grease with cooking spray. Pour in the batter and close the lid.
2. Cook for 5 minutes or until golden-brown, repeat with the remaining batter. Garnish with avocado and bacon before serving.

Per Serving

Calories: **771** | Fat: **67.3g** | Carbs: **6.9g** | Protein: **27.4g**

LOW-CARB EGG MUFFINS

Prep time: **5 minutes** | Cook time: **20 minutes** | Serves **6**

- 6 large free-range eggs
- 65ml unsweetened almond milk
- 65g freshly grated Parmesan cheese
- Sea salt and freshly ground black pepper, to taste

1. Preheat the oven to 180°C (fan 160°C/gas mark 4). Grease a 6-hole muffin tin or line with paper cases.
2. In a medium bowl, whisk together the eggs and almond milk until well combined.
3. Divide the egg mixture evenly between the prepared muffin holes, filling each about three-quarters full.
4. Sprinkle with Parmesan, salt, and pepper. Bake for 15 minutes or until set. Serve hot.

Per Serving

Calories: **78** | Fat: **5.4g** | Protein: **6.9g** | Carbs: **0.6g**

13

CHAPTER 3

AVOCADO AND KALE EGGS

Prep time: **20 minutes** | Cook time: **11 minutes** | Serves **4**

- 5g ghee
- 1 red onion, sliced
- 115g cooking chorizo, sliced into thin rounds
- 250g curly kale, chopped
- 1 ripe avocado, stoned, peeled and chopped
- 4 medium eggs
- Salt and freshly ground black pepper to season

1. Preheat oven to 185°C/165°C fan/Gas mark 4.
2. Melt ghee in a cast-iron frying pan over medium heat and sauté the onion for 2 minutes. Add the chorizo and cook for 2 minutes more, turning once.
3. Add the kale in batches with a splash of water to wilt, season lightly with salt, stir and cook for 3 minutes. Mix in the avocado and turn off the heat.
4. Make four wells in the mixture, crack the eggs into each well, sprinkle with salt and black pepper, and transfer the pan to the preheated oven. Bake for 6 minutes until the egg whites are set but yolks are still runny. Season to taste with salt and pepper, and serve straightaway with low-carb toast.

Per Serving

Calories: **274** | Fat: **23g** | Carbs: **4g** | Protein: **13g**

BACON AND CHEESE FRITTATA

Prep time: **25 minutes** | Cook time: **16 minutes** | Serves **4**

- 10 rashers streaky bacon
- 10 large eggs
- 45g butter, melted
- 125ml almond milk
- Salt and freshly ground black pepper to taste
- 375g mature cheddar cheese, grated
- 65g spring onions, chopped

1. Preheat the oven to 200°C/180°C fan/Gas mark 6 and grease a baking dish with cooking spray. Cook the bacon in a frying pan over medium heat for 6 minutes. Once crispy, remove to kitchen paper and discard the fat. Chop into small pieces. Whisk the eggs, butter, milk, salt, and black pepper. Mix in the bacon and pour the mixture into the baking dish.
2. Sprinkle with cheddar cheese and spring onions, and bake in the oven for 10 minutes or until the eggs are thoroughly cooked. Remove and allow the frittata to cool for 3 minutes, slice into wedges, and serve warm with a dollop of Greek yoghurt.

Per Serving

Calories: **325** | Fat: **28g** | Carbs: **2g** | Protein: **15g**

SPICY EGG MUFFINS WITH BACON & CHEESE

Prep time: **30 minutes** | Cook time: **18 to 20 minutes** | Serves **6**

- 12 medium eggs
- 65ml coconut milk
- Salt and freshly ground black pepper to taste
- 250g mature cheddar cheese, grated
- 12 rashers streaky bacon
- 4 jalapeño chillies, deseeded and finely chopped

1. Preheat oven to 185°C/165°C fan/Gas mark 4.
2. Crack the eggs into a bowl and whisk with coconut milk until combined. Season with salt and pepper, and evenly stir in the cheddar cheese.
3. Line each hole of a muffin tin with a rasher of bacon and fill each with the egg mixture two-thirds full. Top with the jalapeño chillies and bake in the oven for 18 to 20 minutes or until puffed and golden. Remove, allow to cool for a few minutes, and serve with rocket salad.

Per Serving

Calories:**302** | Fat: **23.7g** | Carbs: **3.2g** | Protein: **20g**

BREAKFAST

CAULIFLOWER & CHEESE BURGERS

Prep time: **35 minutes** | Cook time: **20 minutes** | Serves **6**

- 20ml olive oil
- 1 onion, chopped
- 1 garlic clove, crushed
- 450g cauliflower, grated
- 85g coconut flour
- 125g Gruyère cheese, grated
- 250g Parmesan cheese
- 2 medium eggs, beaten
- 1 tsp dried rosemary
- Sea salt and freshly ground black pepper, to taste

1. Set a heavy-based frying pan over medium heat and warm oil. Add garlic and onion and cook until softened, about 3 minutes. Stir in grated cauliflower and cook for a minute; allow to cool and set aside.
2. To the cooled cauliflower, add the remaining ingredients; form balls from the mixture, then press each ball to form a burger patty.
3. Heat oven to 200°C/180°C fan/Gas mark 6 and bake the burgers for 20 minutes. Turn and bake for another 10 minutes or until the top becomes golden brown.

Per Serving

Calories: **416** | Fat: **33.8g** | Carbs: **7.8g** | Protein: **13g**

HAM & EGG BROCCOLI BAKE

Prep time: **25 minutes** | Cook time: **18 to 20 minutes** | Serves **4**

- 2 heads broccoli, cut into small florets
- 2 red peppers, deseeded and chopped
- 65g cooked ham, chopped
- 10g ghee
- 5g dried oregano, plus extra to garnish
- Salt and freshly ground black pepper to taste
- 8 medium eggs

1. Preheat oven to 210°C/190°C fan/Gas mark 7.
2. Melt the ghee in a frying pan over medium heat; brown the ham, stirring frequently, about 3 minutes.
3. Arrange the broccoli, peppers, and ham on a foil-lined baking tray in a single layer, toss to combine; season with salt, oregano, and black pepper. Bake for 10 minutes until the vegetables have softened.
4. Remove, make eight wells with a spoon, and crack an egg into each. Return to the oven and continue to bake for an additional 5 to 7 minutes until the egg whites are set.
5. Season with salt, black pepper, and extra oregano, divide the bake between four plates and serve with strawberry lemonade (optional).

Per Serving

Calories: **344** | Fat: **28g** | Carbs: **4.2g** | Protein: **11g**

CHEESE STUFFED AVOCADOS

Prep time: **20 minutes** | Cook time: **15 to 17 minutes** | Serves **4**

- 3 ripe avocados, halved and stoned, skin left on
- 125g feta cheese, crumbled
- 125g mature cheddar cheese, grated
- 2 medium eggs, beaten
- Salt and freshly ground black pepper, to taste
- 15g fresh basil, chopped

1. Set oven to 180°C/160°C fan/Gas mark 4 and place the avocado halves in an ovenproof dish. In a mixing bowl, combine both cheeses, black pepper, eggs, and salt. Divide the mixture equally between the avocado halves.
2. Bake for 15 to 17 minutes until thoroughly heated. Garnish with fresh basil before serving.

Per Serving

Calories: **342** | Fat: **30.4g** | Carbs: **7.5g** | Protein: **11.1g**

CHAPTER 3

ITALIAN SAUSAGE STACKS

Prep time: 20 minutes | Cook time: 11 minutes | Serves 6

- 6 Italian-style sausage patties
- 60ml olive oil
- 2 ripe avocados, stoned
- 10g fresh lime juice
- Salt and freshly ground black pepper to taste
- 6 fresh medium eggs
- Chilli flakes to garnish

1. In a frying pan, warm the oil over medium heat and fry the sausage patties for about 8 minutes until lightly browned and firm. Remove the patties to a plate.
2. Spoon the avocado into a bowl, mash with the lime juice, and season with salt and black pepper. Spread the mash on the sausages.
3. Bring 750ml of water to the boil in a wide saucepan over high heat, then reduce to a gentle simmer.
4. Crack each egg into a small bowl and gently slip into the simmering water; poach for 2 to 3 minutes. Use a slotted spoon to remove onto kitchen paper to drain. Repeat with the remaining eggs. Top each stack with a poached egg, sprinkle with chilli flakes, salt, black pepper, and snipped chives. Serve with turnip wedges.

Per Serving

Calories: **378** | Fat: **23g** | Carbs: **5g** | Protein: **16g**

CARROT AND COURGETTE LOAF

Prep time: 70 minutes | Cook time: 55 minutes | Serves 4

- 250g carrots, grated
- 250g courgettes, grated and squeezed dry
- 85g coconut flour
- 5g vanilla extract
- 6 medium eggs
- 15ml coconut oil
- ¾ tsp bicarbonate of soda
- 15g ground cinnamon
- 3g salt
- 125g Greek-style yoghurt
- 5ml apple cider vinegar
- 3g ground nutmeg

1. Preheat the oven to 170°C/150°C fan/Gas mark 3 and grease a 900g loaf tin with cooking spray. Set aside.
2. Mix the carrots, courgettes, coconut flour, vanilla extract, eggs, coconut oil, bicarbonate of soda, ground cinnamon, salt, yoghurt, vinegar, and nutmeg. Pour the batter into the loaf tin and bake for 55 minutes.
3. Remove the loaf and leave to cool for 5 minutes. Store and use for toast, sandwiches, or serve with soups and salads.

Per Serving

Calories:**175** | Fat: **10.5g** | Carbs: **1.8g** | Protein: **11.6g**

MASCARPONE & VANILLA BREAKFAST CUPS

Prep time: 20 minutes | Cook time: 12 to 15 minutes | Serves 6

- 185g mascarpone cheese
- 65g natural yoghurt
- 3 medium eggs, beaten
- 15g walnuts, ground
- 55g erythritol
- 3g vanilla extract
- 5g ground cinnamon

1. Heat oven to 180°C/160°C fan/Gas mark 4 and grease a muffin tin. Mix all ingredients in a bowl.
2. Divide the mixture between the muffin holes. Bake for 12 to 15 minutes. Remove and place on a wire rack to cool slightly before serving.

Per Serving

Calories:**181** | Fat: **13.5g** | Carbs: **3.7g** | Protein: **10.5g**

BREAKFAST

SMOKED HAM AND EGG MUFFINS

Prep time: **40 minutes** | Cook time: **25 minutes** | Serves **9**

- 500g smoked ham, chopped
- 85g Parmesan cheese, grated
- 65g ground almonds
- 9 medium eggs
- 85g mayonnaise, sugar-free
- 1g garlic powder
- 65g onion, chopped
- Sea salt to taste

1. Preheat your oven to 185°C/165°C fan/Gas mark 5.
2. Lightly grease nine holes of a muffin tin with cooking spray and set aside. Place the onion, ham, garlic powder, and salt in a food processor and pulse until finely ground. Stir in the mayonnaise, ground almonds, and Parmesan cheese. Press this mixture into the muffin holes.
3. Ensure the mixture lines the sides of each hole to create space for the egg. Bake for 5 minutes. Crack an egg into each muffin hole. Return to the oven and bake for 20 more minutes or until the tops are firm to the touch and eggs are set. Leave to cool slightly before serving.

Per Serving

Calories:**367** | Fat: **28g** | Carbs: **1g** | Protein: **13.5g**

NUTTY 'PORRIDGE'

Prep time:**10 minutes** | Cook time: **8 hours** | Serves **6**

- 15ml coconut oil
- 250ml coconut milk
- 250g desiccated coconut, unsweetened
- 125g pecans, chopped
- 125g flaked almonds
- 65g granulated erythritol
- 1 ripe avocado, diced
- 60g protein powder
- 5g ground cinnamon
- 1g ground nutmeg
- 125g blueberries, to garnish

1. Lightly grease the bowl of a slow cooker with the coconut oil.
2. Place the coconut milk, desiccated coconut, pecans, flaked almonds, erythritol, avocado, protein powder, cinnamon, and nutmeg in the slow cooker.
3. Cover and cook on low for 8 hours.
4. Stir the mixture to achieve the desired consistency.
5. Serve topped with the blueberries.

Per Serving

Calories: **365** | Fat: **33g** | Protein: **14g** | Carbs: **10g**

SPICED AVOCADO EGG BOATS

Prep time: **20 minutes** | Cook time: **17 minutes** | Serves **4**

- 2 tablespoons olive oil
- 4 ripe avocados, halved lengthways and stoned
- 250g mature Cheddar cheese, grated
- 4 large free-range eggs, beaten
- 1 teaspoon chilli powder
- Sea salt and freshly ground black pepper
- 15g fresh basil leaves, chopped

1. Preheat the oven to 180°C (fan 160°C/gas mark 4).
2. In a bowl, combine the grated cheese, chilli powder, beaten eggs, salt, and pepper.
3. Carefully spoon the mixture into the avocado halves, dividing equally.
4. Bake for 15-17 minutes until the eggs are set.
5. Scatter with fresh basil before serving.

Per Serving

Calories: **355** | Fat: **29g** | Carbs: **6.9g** | Protein: **12g**

CHAPTER 3

TOFU SCRAMBLED WITH TOMATOES & MUSHROOMS

Prep time: **20 minutes** | Cook time: **5 minutes** | Serves **4**

- 5 medium eggs
- 15g butter
- 250g mushrooms, sliced
- 2 cloves garlic, crushed
- 450g firm tofu, crumbled
- Salt and freshly ground black pepper to taste
- 1 tomato, chopped
- 30g sesame seeds

1. Melt the butter in a frying pan over medium heat, and sauté the mushrooms for 5 minutes until tender. Add the garlic and cook for 1 minute. Crumble the tofu into the pan, season with salt and pepper. Cook for 6 minutes, stirring continuously. Add the tomato and cook until softened, about 5 minutes.
2. Whisk eggs in a bowl and pour over the tomato mixture. Use a wooden spoon to immediately stir the eggs while cooking until scrambled and set, 5 minutes. Sprinkle with sesame seeds, and serve.

Per Serving

Calories: **315** | Fat: **22g** | Carbs:**4.5g** | Protein: **25.5g**

BROCCOLI & CHEDDAR FRITTATA

Prep time: **20 minutes** | Cook time: **12 minutes** | Serves **4**

- 1 tbsp olive oil
- 125g onions, chopped
- 250g broccoli, chopped
- 8 medium eggs, beaten
- 3g jalapeño chilli, finely chopped
- Salt and chilli powder, to taste
- 185g mature cheddar cheese, grated
- 65g fresh basil, to serve

1. Set an ovenproof frying pan over medium heat and warm the oil. Add onions and sauté until caramelised. Add the broccoli and cook until tender. Add jalapeño chilli and eggs; season with chilli powder and salt. Cook until the eggs begin to set.
2. Scatter cheddar cheese over the frittata. Heat oven to 185°C/165°C fan/Gas mark 5 and cook for approximately 12 minutes, until frittata is set in the middle. Cut into wedges and garnish with fresh basil before serving.

Per Serving

Calories: **248** | Fat: **17.1g** | Carbs: **6.2g** | Protein: **17.6g**

CHOCOLATE PROTEIN COCONUT SHAKE

Prep time: **4 minutes** | Cook time: **2 minutes** | Serves **4**

- 750ml flaxseed milk, chilled
- 3 teaspoons unsweetened cocoa powder
- 1 medium ripe avocado, stoned and peeled
- 250ml coconut milk, chilled
- 3 fresh mint leaves, plus extra to garnish
- 42g erythritol (or sweetener of choice)
- 1 tablespoon low-carb protein powder
- Whipped cream, to serve

1. Place the flaxseed milk, cocoa powder, avocado, coconut milk, mint leaves, erythritol, and protein powder into a blender. Blend for 1 minute until completely smooth.
2. Pour into serving glasses and top each with a dollop of whipped cream. Garnish with fresh mint leaves and serve straightaway.

Per Serving

Calories: **265** | Fat: **15.5g** | Carbs: **4g** | Protein: **12g**

BREAKFAST

HUEVOS RANCHEROS

Prep time: **10 minutes** | Cook time: **3 hours** | Serves **8**

- 15ml extra virgin olive oil
- 10 medium eggs
- 250ml double cream
- 250g Monterey Jack cheese, grated, divided
- 250g prepared or homemade salsa
- 1 spring onion, green and white parts, chopped
- 1 jalapeño chilli, chopped
- 3g chilli powder
- 3g salt
- 1 ripe avocado, chopped, for garnish
- 15g fresh basil, chopped, for garnish

1. Lightly grease the bowl of the slow cooker with the olive oil.
2. In a large bowl, whisk together the eggs, double cream, 125g of the cheese, salsa, spring onion, jalapeño, chilli powder, and salt. Pour the mixture into the slow cooker and sprinkle the top with the remaining 125g of cheese.
3. Cover and cook until the eggs are firm, about 3 hours on low.
4. Let the eggs cool slightly, then cut into wedges and serve garnished with avocado and basil.

Per Serving

Calories: **302** | Fat: **26g** | Protein: **13g** | Carbs: **5g**

RICOTTA CLOUD PANCAKES WITH WHIPPED CREAM

Prep time: **10 minutes** | Cook time: **1 minutes** | Serves **4**

- 250g ground almonds
- 5g baking powder
- 35g granulated sweetener
- 5g salt
- 300g ricotta cheese
- 85ml coconut milk
- 2 large eggs
- 250ml double cream, whipped

1. In a medium bowl, whisk the ground almonds, baking powder, sweetener, and salt. Set aside.
2. Crack the eggs into the blender and process on medium speed for 30 seconds. Add the ricotta cheese, continue processing, and gradually pour in the coconut milk while blending. In about 90 seconds, the mixture will be creamy and smooth. Pour into the dry ingredients and whisk to combine.
3. Set a frying pan over medium heat and let it heat for a minute. Then, drop a tablespoonful of mixture into the pan and cook for 1 minute.
4. Turn the pancake and cook for a further minute. Remove to a plate and repeat the cooking process until all the batter is used. Serve the pancakes with whipped cream.

Per Serving

Calories: **407** | Fat: **30.6g** | Carbs: **6.6g** | Protein: **11.5g**

LETTUCE CUPS WITH MUSHROOMS AND GRUYÈRE

Prep time: **20 minutes** | Cook time: **8 minutes** | Serves **4**

- 2 tablespoons olive oil
- 1 small onion, finely chopped
- 250g chestnut mushrooms, finely chopped
- Pinch of cayenne pepper
- Sea salt and freshly ground black pepper
- 4 large Little Gem lettuce leaves
- 4 slices Gruyère cheese
- 1 ripe tomato, thinly sliced

1. Heat the olive oil in a large frying pan over medium-high heat. Gently fry the onion for 3 minutes until softened.
2. Add the mushrooms and cayenne pepper, cooking for 4-5 minutes until tender. Season well with salt and pepper.
3. Arrange the lettuce leaves on serving plates. Fill with the mushroom mixture and top with tomato slices and Gruyère.

Per Serving

Calories: **481** | Fat: **42g** | Carbs: **5.7g** | Protein: **20g**

CHAPTER 3

ASPARAGUS & GOAT CHEESE OMELET

Prep time: **10 minutes** | Cook time: **6 minutes** | Serves **4**

- 2 tablespoons olive oil (30ml)
- 1 bunch asparagus, trimmed and chopped
- 1 spring onion, finely chopped
- 8 large free-range eggs, beaten
- 5g fresh rosemary, finely chopped
- 5g fresh flat-leaf parsley, chopped
- Sea salt and freshly ground black pepper
- 250g soft goat's cheese, crumbled

1. Heat the olive oil in a large non-stick frying pan over medium heat. Gently cook the asparagus and spring onion for 4-5 minutes until tender.
2. Pour in the beaten eggs and sprinkle with parsley, black pepper, salt, and rosemary.
3. Once the eggs begin to set, scatter the goat's cheese over one half of the omelette. Using a spatula, carefully fold the other half over the filling. Cook for another minute until just set through. Serve immediately.

Per Serving

Calories: **410** | Fat: **28.1g** | Carbs: **2.5g** | Protein: **24.3g**

TURKEY AND CHEESE EGG BITES

Prep time: **5 minutes** | Cook time: **35 minutes** | Serves **6**

- 6 large free-range eggs
- 65ml unsweetened almond milk
- Pinch of sea salt and freshly ground black pepper
- 125g mature Cheddar cheese, grated
- 2 slices free-range turkey breast, diced

1. Preheat the oven to 175°C (fan 155°C/gas mark 3). Grease a 6-hole muffin tin or line with paper cases.
2. In a medium bowl, whisk together the eggs, almond milk, salt, and pepper until well combined.
3. Divide the egg mixture evenly between the prepared muffin holes, filling each about three-quarters full.
4. Sprinkle the grated cheese and diced turkey evenly among the muffin holes.
5. Bake for 25-30 minutes, or until set. Serve hot.

Per Serving

Calories: **116** | Fat: **7.3g** | Protein: **12.4g** | Carbs: **1.2g**

SPINACH SALAD WITH GOAT CHEESE & PINE NUTS

Prep time: **20 minutes** | Cook time: **5 minutes** | Serves **4**

- 500g baby spinach leaves
- 125g pine nuts, lightly toasted
- 350g hard goat's cheese, finely grated
- 2 tablespoons white wine vinegar (30ml)
- 2 tablespoons extra virgin olive oil (30ml)
- Sea salt and freshly ground black pepper, to taste

1. Preheat the oven to 190°C (fan 170°C/gas mark 5). Divide the grated goat's cheese into two equal circles on two pieces of baking parchment.
2. Bake for 10 minutes until golden and bubbling.
3. Immediately drape the parchment papers over upturned bowls to create cheese baskets. Leave to cool and crisp up for 15 minutes.
4. Divide the spinach between serving plates, season with salt and pepper, and drizzle with vinegar and olive oil. Top with toasted pine nuts and the goat's cheese crisps.

Per Serving

Calories: **410** | Fat: **31.2g** | Carbs: **3.4g** | Protein: **27g**

BREAKFAST

BREAKFAST FRITTATA

Prep time: **5 minutes** | Cook time: **30 minutes** | Serves **6**

- 2 organic chicken sausages (no added sugar), diced
- 250g fresh spinach
- 125g asparagus, chopped
- 6 large eggs
- 2 tablespoons unsweetened almond milk
- 125g cherry tomatoes, halved
- 250g organic mozzarella, grated

1. Preheat the oven to 190°C/170°C fan/Gas mark 5.
2. Brown the chicken sausages in a cast-iron frying pan or ovenproof pan.
3. Add the spinach and asparagus to the pan and cook for 2 minutes, or until the spinach has wilted.
4. Whisk together the eggs and almond milk. Stir in the tomatoes.
5. Pour the egg mixture into the pan and bake the frittata for 20 to 22 minutes, or until the eggs are set.
6. Remove the frittata and sprinkle with the mozzarella. Cut into wedges and serve. Store in an airtight container in the fridge for up to 4 days.

Per Serving

Calories: **134** | Fat: **7.3g** | Protein: **13.2g** | Carbs: **4.7g**

CHEESE CIABATTA WITH PEPPERONI

Prep time: **30 minutes** | Cook time: **2 minutes** | Serves **6**

- 280g cream cheese, softened
- 625g mozzarella cheese, grated
- 4 large free-range eggs, beaten
- 42g Pecorino Romano cheese, finely grated
- 125g pork scratchings, finely crushed
- 2 teaspoons baking powder
- 125g passata
- 12 large slices pepperoni

1. In a large bowl, combine the beaten eggs, grated mozzarella, and softened cream cheese. Fold in the baking powder, crushed pork scratchings, and Pecorino Romano cheese. Shape the mixture into 6 ciabatta-shaped portions.
2. Heat a non-stick frying pan over medium heat. Cook each ciabatta for 2 minutes on each side until golden brown and cheese is melted.
3. Top each ciabatta with a spoonful of passata and pepperoni slices. Serve hot.

Per Serving

Calories: **464** | Fat: **33.6g** | Carbs: **9.1g** | Protein: **31.1g**

CHIA SEED AND STRAWBERRY PUDDING

Prep time: **5 minutes** | Cook time: **5 minutes** | Serves **4**

- 20 fresh strawberries
- 800ml unsweetened almond milk
- 5ml vanilla extract
- 180ml double cream
- 60g chia seeds
- 4 teaspoons liquid stevia
- Handful of walnuts, roughly chopped, to serve
- 4 fresh mint leaves, to garnish

1. In a medium bowl, crush 8 strawberries with a fork until puréed. Add the almond milk, double cream, chia seeds, and liquid stevia. Stir well to combine.
2. Cover and refrigerate overnight to set.
3. Slice the remaining strawberries. Divide the pudding between serving glasses and top with strawberry slices, chopped walnuts, and mint leaves.

Per Serving

Calories: **532** | Fat: **42g** | Carbs:**5.3g** | Protein: **14g**

CHAPTER 3

BELGIAN-STYLE WAFFLES WITH LEMON CREAM CHEESE

Prep time: **25 minutes** | Cook time: **10 minutes** | Serves **4**

- 250g full-fat cream cheese, softened
- Zest and juice of 1 unwaxed lemon
- 30g stevia
- For the waffles:
- 3 tablespoons olive oil
- 250ml unsweetened almond milk
- 4 large free-range eggs
- 250g ground almonds
- Low-calorie cooking spray

1. For the spread, beat together the cream cheese, lemon zest, lemon juice, and stevia until smooth. Set aside.
2. In a large bowl, whisk together the olive oil, almond milk, and eggs. Fold in the ground almonds until smooth. Leave to stand for 5 minutes to thicken.
3. Heat your waffle maker and spray with low-calorie cooking spray.
4. Pour about 65g of batter into the waffle maker and cook for approximately 5 minutes until golden.
5. Cut the waffles into quarters, spread with the lemon cream cheese, and sandwich together to serve.

Per Serving

Calories: **322** | Fat: **26g** | Carbs: **7.7g** | Protein: **11g**

SESAME & POPPY SEED BAGELS

Prep time: **25 minutes** | Cook time: **20 minutes** | Serves **4**

- 125g coconut flour
- 6 large free-range eggs
- 125ml water
- 125g ground flaxseed
- 1 teaspoon onion powder
- 1 teaspoon garlic powder
- 5g dried oregano
- 5g sesame seeds
- 5g poppy seeds

1. Preheat the oven to 180°C (fan 160°C/gas mark 4). Lightly grease a 4-hole doughnut tin.
2. In a large bowl, combine the coconut flour, eggs, water, ground flaxseed, onion powder, garlic powder, and oregano until well mixed.
3. Divide the mixture between the prepared tin holes. Sprinkle evenly with poppy and sesame seeds.
4. Bake for 20 minutes until firm and lightly golden.
5. Cool on a wire rack for 5 minutes before serving.

Per Serving

Calories: **431** | Fat: **20g** | Carbs: **1.3g** | Protein: **29g**

KALE AND BROCCOLI SLAW WITH CRISPY BACON

Prep time: **10 minutes** | Cook time: **5 minutes** | Serves **4**

- 2 tablespoons olive oil
- 250g broccoli slaw
- 250g kale, finely shredded
- 2 rashers streaky bacon, finely chopped
- 30g Parmesan cheese, freshly grated
- 5g celery seeds
- 2 tablespoons cider vinegar
- Sea salt and freshly ground black pepper

1. Dry-fry the bacon in a frying pan over medium heat until crispy, about 5 minutes. Remove with a slotted spoon and set aside to cool.
2. In a large serving bowl, combine the broccoli slaw, shredded kale, and celery seeds.
3. Drizzle with olive oil and cider vinegar, then season well with salt and pepper. Toss thoroughly to combine.
4. Top with the crispy bacon and freshly grated Parmesan. Serve immediately.

Per Serving

Calories: **305** | Fat: **26.9g** | Carbs: **3.2g** | Protein: **7.3g**

CHAPTER 4: SNACKS AND APPETIZERS

CHAPTER 4

MUSHROOM AND BACON ROLLS

Prep time: 5 minutes | Cook time: 45 minutes | Serves 5

- For the rolls:
- 225g enoki mushrooms
- 5 rashers streaky bacon, halved lengthways
- For the dipping sauce:
- 125ml water
- 2 tablespoons sesame oil
- 2 tablespoons coconut aminos
- 5g monk fruit sweetener
- 1 large garlic clove, crushed
- ¼ teaspoon ground ginger
- 5g Chinese five-spice powder
- Sea salt and freshly ground black pepper

1. Preheat the oven to 190°C (fan 170°C/gas mark 5). Line a baking tray with baking parchment.
2. Wrap each portion of mushrooms with bacon and secure with a wooden cocktail stick.
3. Place on the prepared tray and bake for 40 minutes, turning halfway through, until the bacon is crispy.
4. Meanwhile, make the sauce: combine all sauce ingredients in a small saucepan over medium heat. Simmer until reduced and thickened.
5. Serve the bacon rolls hot with the dipping sauce alongside.

Per Serving

Calories: **323** | Fat: **33.2g** | Carbs: **4.4g** | Protein: **1.5g**

GARLIC AND HERB BUTTER EGGS

Prep time: 15 minutes | Cook time: 10 minutes | Serves 4

- 1 tablespoon coconut oil
- 30g unsalted butter
- 5g fresh thyme leaves
- 4 large free-range eggs
- 2 garlic cloves, crushed
- 125g fresh flat-leaf parsley, chopped
- 125g fresh basil, chopped
- 1 teaspoon ground cumin
- 1 teaspoon cayenne pepper
- Sea salt and freshly ground black pepper

1. Heat the coconut oil and butter in a large frying pan over medium heat.
2. Add garlic and thyme, cooking for 30 seconds until fragrant.
3. Add parsley and basil, cooking for 2-3 minutes until crisp.
4. Carefully crack the eggs into the pan. Reduce heat and cook for 4-6 minutes until set to your liking.
5. Season with cumin, cayenne, salt, and pepper.
6. Transfer to warm plates and serve immediately.

Per Serving

Calories: **321** | Carbs: **2.5g** | Fat: **21.5g** | Protein: **12.8g**

DILL PICKLES WITH TUNA MAYO

Prep time: 40 minutes | Cook time: 5 minutes | Serves 12

- 500g canned tuna, drained
- 6 large dill pickles
- 1g garlic powder
- 85g sugar-free mayonnaise
- 14g dried onion flakes

1. In a bowl, combine the mayonnaise, tuna, onion flakes, and garlic powder.
2. Slice the pickles in half lengthwise and top each half with a portion of the tuna mixture. Chill in the fridge for 30 minutes before serving.

Per Serving

Calories: **118** | Fat: **10g** | Carbs: **1.5g** | Protein: **11g**

SNACKS AND APPETIZERS

HAM AND AVOCADO DEVILLED EGGS

Prep time: **5 minutes** | Cook time: **20 minutes** | Serves **4**

- 4 large free-range eggs
- ½ ripe avocado, mashed
- ¼ teaspoon English mustard
- 1 garlic clove, crushed
- 60g cooked ham, finely chopped

1. Place the eggs in a saucepan and cover with cold water. Bring to the boil, then remove from heat, cover, and leave for 12 minutes.
2. Drain and cool under cold running water. Peel and halve the eggs lengthways.
3. Remove the yolks and mix with the mashed avocado, mustard, and garlic.
4. Spoon the mixture back into the egg whites and top with chopped ham.

Per Serving

Calories: **128** | Fat: **8.9g** | Carbs: **2.9g** | Protein: **9.2g**

SPICY GLAZED SPARE RIBS

Prep time: **5 minutes** | Cook time: **2 hours 35 minutes** | Serves **4**

- 900g pork spare ribs
- 15g fajita seasoning
- 2 garlic cloves, crushed
- 125ml chicken stock
- 250g passata

1. Preheat the oven to 130°C (fan 110°C/gas mark ½).
2. In a large bowl, combine the fajita seasoning, garlic, stock, and passata.
3. Coat the ribs thoroughly in the mixture.
4. Arrange on a foil-lined baking tray.
5. Bake for 2½ hours until tender.
6. Turn the grill to high and grill for 5-8 minutes until the sauce is sticky and caramelised.

Per Serving

Calories: **344** | Fat: **13.6g** | Carbs: **4.9g** | Protein: **49.5g**

CHEESY GARLIC SCONES

Prep time: **20 minutes** | Cook time: **12 minutes** | Serves **4**

- 85g ground almonds
- 10g garlic granules
- Salt, to taste
- 5g baking powder
- 5 medium eggs
- 85g unsalted butter, melted
- 300g mature Cheddar, grated
- 85g Greek yoghurt

1. Preheat the oven to 170°C/150°C fan/Gas mark 3.
2. In a large mixing bowl, combine the ground almonds, garlic granules, salt, baking powder and grated Cheddar.
3. In a separate bowl, whisk together the eggs, melted butter and Greek yoghurt. Pour this wet mixture into the dry ingredients. Stir thoroughly until you achieve a thick, scone-like consistency. Using a dessert spoon, drop mounds of the mixture onto a lined baking tray, leaving 5cm gaps between each scone.
4. Bake for 12 minutes, or until golden brown and well-risen.

Per Serving

Calories:**153** | Fat: **14.2g** | Carbs: **1.4g** | Protein: **5.4g**

CHAPTER 4

DEVILLED EGGS WITH SPICY MAYO

Prep time: **15 minutes** | Cook time: **10 minutes** | Serves **4**

- 8 large free-range eggs
- 750ml water
- Bowl of iced water
- 42g Sriracha sauce
- 56g mayonnaise
- Salt, to taste
- 1g smoked paprika

1. Place the eggs in a saucepan and cover with water. Bring to the boil over high heat, then reduce to a gentle simmer for 10 minutes. Immediately plunge the eggs into the iced water and leave until completely cold. Carefully peel away the shells.
2. Halve the eggs lengthways and gently remove the yolks into a bowl. Mash the yolks with a fork, then mix in the Sriracha sauce, mayonnaise and half the paprika until smooth. Spoon or pipe the mixture back into the egg whites, creating a slight dome.
3. Dust with the remaining paprika and serve.

Per Serving

Calories: **195** | Fat: **19g** | Carbs: **1g** | Protein: **4g**

CRISPY GREEN BEAN AND CHEESE STRAWS

Prep time: **30 minutes** | Cook time: **15 minutes** | Serves **6**

- 65g Pecorino Romano cheese, finely grated
- 65g pork scratching crumbs
- 5g garlic granules
- Salt and freshly ground black pepper, to taste
- 2 medium eggs
- 450g green beans, topped and tailed

1. Preheat the oven to 210°C/190°C fan/Gas mark 7. Line two baking trays with foil and lightly grease.
2. In a shallow dish, combine the Pecorino, pork scratching crumbs, garlic granules, salt and pepper. In a separate bowl, beat the eggs.
3. Dip each green bean in beaten egg, then coat in the cheese mixture. Arrange in a single layer on the prepared baking trays.
4. Lightly mist with cooking spray and bake for 15 minutes until crispy.
5. Transfer to a wire rack to cool slightly. Serve warm with sugar-free tomato relish.

Per Serving

Calories: **210** | Fat: **19g** | Carbs: **3g** | Protein: **5g**

STRAWBERRY CHOCOLATE MOUSSE

Prep time: **30 minutes** | Cook time: **30 minutes** | Serves **4**

- 6 large eggs
- 250g dark chocolate chips
- 500ml double cream
- 500g fresh strawberries, sliced
- 1 tsp vanilla extract
- 14g xylitol

1. In a heatproof bowl, melt the chocolate in the microwave on high for 1 minute, then let it cool for 10 minutes.
2. In a mixing bowl, whip the double cream until soft peaks form. Add the eggs, vanilla extract, and xylitol, whisking until combined. Gently fold in the cooled chocolate.
3. Spoon the mousse into serving glasses, top with strawberry slices, and refrigerate for at least 30 minutes before serving.

Per Serving

Calories: **567** | Fat: **45.6g** | Carbs: **9.6g** | Protein: **13.6g**

SNACKS AND APPETIZERS

SPICY CHICKEN AND CUCUMBER CANAPÉS

Prep time: **5 minutes** | Cook time: **5 minutes** | Serves **6**

- 2 cucumbers, cut into 2.5cm thick rounds
- 500g cooked chicken, finely diced
- 1 small green chilli, deseeded and finely chopped
- 14g Dijon mustard
- 85g mayonnaise
- Salt and freshly ground black pepper, to taste

1. Using a small knife or melon baller, hollow out the centre of each cucumber round to create a small well. Set aside.
2. In a bowl, combine the diced chicken, chopped chilli, Dijon mustard, mayonnaise, salt and pepper until evenly mixed.
3. Fill each cucumber cup with the chicken mixture and arrange on a serving platter.

Per Serving

Calories: 170 | Fat: **14g** | Carbs: **0g** | Protein: **10g**

GARLIC AND BASIL MASHED CELERIAC

Prep time: **30 minutes** | Cook time: **15 minutes** | Serves **4**

- 900g celeriac, peeled and chopped
- 1 litre water
- 60g cream cheese
- 28g butter
- 85g sour cream
- 3g garlic powder
- 10g dried basil
- Salt and black pepper, to taste

1. Place the celeriac in a pot, cover with water, and bring to a boil over high heat. Reduce heat to low and simmer for 15 minutes, then drain.
2. In a large mixing bowl, add the drained celeriac, cream cheese, butter, sour cream, garlic powder, dried basil, salt, and pepper. Use a hand mixer on medium speed to blend until smooth. Serve warm.

Per Serving

Calories: **94** | Fat: **0.5g** | Carbs: **6g** | Protein: **2.4g**

CHEESY CAULIFLOWER GRATIN

Prep time: **27 minutes** | Cook time: **28 minutes** | Serves **6**

- 2 heads cauliflower, cut into florets
- 65g unsalted butter, melted
- Salt and freshly ground black pepper, to taste
- 1 pinch dried chilli flakes
- 125g mayonnaise
- 1 tsp Dijon mustard
- 42g Pecorino cheese, finely grated

1. Preheat the oven to 200°C/180°C fan/Gas mark 6. Lightly grease a baking dish.
2. In a large bowl, toss the cauliflower florets with melted butter, salt, pepper and chilli flakes until well coated. In a separate small bowl, mix together the mayonnaise and Dijon mustard for the sauce.
3. Arrange the seasoned cauliflower in the prepared baking dish. Sprinkle evenly with the grated Pecorino.
4. Bake for 25-28 minutes, until the cheese has melted and turned golden brown.
5. Allow to rest for 3 minutes before serving with the mayonnaise sauce.

Per Serving

Calories: **363** | Fat: **35g** | Carbs: **2g** | Protein: **6g**

CHAPTER 4

ROASTED MIXED NUTS

Prep time: 5 minutes | **Cook time:** 20 minutes | **Serves** 4

- 250g raw pecans
- 250g raw cashews
- 250g raw almonds
- 250g raw walnuts
- 3 tablespoons coconut oil, melted
- 14g sea salt
- 5g cayenne pepper (optional)

1. Preheat the oven to 175°C (fan 155°C). Line a baking tray with parchment paper.
2. In a mixing bowl, toss all the ingredients until the nuts are evenly coated with oil.
3. Spread the nuts out on the baking tray and bake for 14 to 16 minutes, or until they are lightly browned and fragrant. Remove from the oven and allow to cool. Store in a glass container at room temperature.

Per Serving

Calories: 674 | **Fat:** 62.2g | **Protein:** 18.6g | **Carbs:** 20.6g

EASIEST KETO CHEESECAKE EVER

Prep time: 5 minutes | **Cook time:** 35 minutes | **Serves** 6

- 185g coconut flour
- 80ml butter, at room temperature
- 450g cream cheese, at room temperature
- 170g sour cream
- 125g erythritol

1. For the crust, mix the coconut flour with the butter until combined. Press the mixture into the bottom of a lightly greased baking tin and refrigerate.
2. For the filling, mix the cream cheese, sour cream, and erythritol until smooth. Pour the filling over the prepared crust.
3. Bake in a preheated oven at 225°C for 10 minutes, then reduce the temperature to 180°C and bake for an additional 20 minutes.
4. Chill well before serving.

Per Serving

Calories: 411 | **Fat:** 38g | **Carbs:** 7.5g | **Protein:** 5.8g

JALAPENO TURKEY TOMATO BITES

Prep time: 5 minutes | **Cook time:** 5 minutes | **Serves** 4

- 4 medium tomatoes, sliced
- 250g chopped turkey ham
- ¼ jalapeño pepper, finely minced
- 42g Dijon mustard
- 65g mayonnaise
- Salt and black pepper, to taste
- 14g fresh parsley, chopped

1. In a bowl, combine the turkey ham, jalapeño, mustard, mayonnaise, salt, and black pepper.
2. Arrange tomato slices on a serving platter, then divide the turkey mixture evenly between them. Garnish with parsley and serve.

Per Serving

Calories: 245 | **Fat:** 15.3g | **Carbs:** 6.3g | **Protein:** 21g

SNACKS AND APPETIZERS

COCOA NUTS GOJI BARS

Prep time: **5 minutes** | Cook time: **5 minutes** | Serves **6**

- 250g raw almonds
- 250g raw walnuts
- 1g cinnamon powder
- 65g dried goji berries
- 3g vanilla extract
- 28g unsweetened chocolate chips
- 28ml coconut oil
- 14g golden flaxseed meal
- 5g erythritol

1. In a food processor, blend the walnuts and almonds until smooth. Add the cinnamon, goji berries, vanilla extract, chocolate chips, coconut oil, flaxseed meal, and erythritol. Process until the mixture is sticky, about 2 minutes.
2. Spread a large piece of cling film on a flat surface, place the mixture on it, and use a rolling pin to flatten it into a thick rectangle. Unwrap, then cut into bars with a knife lightly coated with oil.

Per Serving

Calories: 170 | Fat: **11g** | Carbs: **6g** | Protein: **2g**

KETO COOKIE DOUGH BARS

Prep time: **5 minutes** | Cook time: **30 minutes** | Serves **6**

- 160g cashew or almond butter
- 125g unsweetened chocolate chips
- 2 scoops vanilla bone broth protein
- 3 tablespoons coconut cream
- 1 large egg

1. Preheat the oven to 160°C (fan 140°C). Line a baking tray with parchment paper.
2. Place all the ingredients in a food processor and blend until smooth. Stop to scrape down the sides, then blend again.
3. Transfer the dough to the prepared baking tray. Use a rolling pin to shape it into a rectangle about ¼ inch thick.
4. Bake for 20 minutes, then remove from the oven and allow to cool completely.
5. Cut into six bars and store in the refrigerator.

Per Serving

Calories: **281** | Fat: **20.6g** | Protein: **12.8g** | Carbs: **11.5g**

FRIDAY NIGHT CAULIFLOWER FRITTERS

Prep time: **35 minutes** | Cook time: **3 minutes** | Serves **4**

- 450g grated cauliflower
- 125g grated Parmesan cheese
- 85g onion, finely chopped
- 3g baking powder
- 125g almond flour
- 3 large eggs
- 3ml lemon juice
- Olive oil, for frying
- Salt, to taste

1. Sprinkle salt over the grated cauliflower in a bowl and let it sit for 10 minutes. Add the remaining ingredients to the bowl and mix with your hands until well combined.
2. Heat a skillet over medium heat and add a small amount of olive oil. Shape the cauliflower mixture into fritters.
3. Fry each fritter for about 3 minutes per side until golden brown. Serve warm.

Per Serving

Calories: **69** | Carbs: **3g** | Fat: **5.3g** | Protein: **4.5g**

CHAPTER 4

HOMEMADE CHEESY SPINACH BALLS

Prep time: 30 minutes | Cook time: 12 minutes | Serves 8

- 80g ricotta cheese, crumbled
- 1g nutmeg
- 1g black pepper
- 42g heavy cream
- 5g garlic powder
- 14g onion powder
- 28ml melted butter
- 80g grated Parmesan cheese
- 2 large eggs
- 225g spinach, blanched and chopped
- 250g almond flour

1. Place all the ingredients in a food processor and process until smooth. Place the mixture in the freezer for about 10 minutes to firm up.
2. Roll the mixture into balls and arrange them on a lined baking tray.
3. Bake at 175°C (fan 155°C) for 10-12 minutes until golden brown.

Per Serving

Calories: **60** | Carbs: **0.8g** | Fat: **5g** | Protein: **2g**

EASY SALAD WITH BACON AND AVOCADO

Prep time: 20 minutes | Cook time: 5 minutes | Serves 4

- 2 large avocados (1 chopped, 1 sliced for garnish)
- 1 spring onion, sliced
- 4 cooked bacon rashers, crumbled
- 500g fresh spinach
- 2 small lettuce heads, chopped
- 2 hard-boiled eggs, chopped

For the Vinaigrette:

- 42ml olive oil
- 5g Dijon mustard
- 14ml apple cider vinegar

1. In a large bowl, combine the spinach, lettuce, eggs, chopped avocado, and spring onion.
2. In a separate bowl, whisk together the vinaigrette ingredients. Pour the dressing over the salad and toss to combine.
3. Top with the sliced avocado and crumbled bacon. Serve immediately and enjoy!

Per Serving

Calories:**350** | Carbs:**3.4g** | Fat: **33g** | Protein: **7g**

BAKED HAM & CHEESE EGG CAKES

Prep time: 35 minutes | Cook time: 25 minutes | Serves 8

- 500g ham, chopped
- 80g grated Parmesan cheese
- 14g fresh parsley, chopped
- 65g almond flour
- 9 large eggs
- 80g sugar-free mayonnaise
- 1g garlic powder
- 65g onion, chopped
- Sea salt, to taste
- Cooking spray

1. Preheat the oven to 187°C (fan 167°C). Lightly grease nine muffin tins with cooking spray and set aside.
2. In a food processor, pulse together the onion, ham, garlic powder, and salt until finely chopped.
3. Stir in the mayonnaise, almond flour, and Parmesan cheese, then press this mixture into the muffin cups.
4. Bake for 5 minutes, then crack an egg into each muffin cup. Return to the oven and bake for an additional 20 minutes, or until the tops are firm and the eggs are cooked. Allow to cool slightly before serving.

Per Serving

Calories: **267** | Carbs: **1g** | Fat: **18g** | Protein: **13.5g**

SNACKS AND APPETIZERS

GREEK SALAD WITH CAPERS

Prep time: **10 minutes** | Cook time: **5 minutes** | Serves **4**

- 5 tomatoes, chopped
- 1 large cucumber, chopped
- 1 green pepper, chopped
- 1 small red onion, chopped
- 16 Kalamata olives, chopped
- 56g capers
- 200g feta cheese, chopped
- 5g dried oregano
- 56ml olive oil
- Salt, to taste

1. In a large bowl, combine the tomatoes, cucumber, pepper, onion, feta, and olives. Season with salt to taste.
2. In a small bowl, mix together the capers, olive oil, and oregano. Drizzle over the salad and serve.

Per Serving

Calories: **323** | Carbs: **8g** | Fat: **28g** | Protein: **9.3g**

CHOCOLATE CHIP COOKIES

Prep time: **20 minutes** | Cook time: **15 minutes** | Serves **4**

- 250g unsalted butter, softened
- 500g Swerve brown sugar
- 3 large eggs
- 500g almond flour
- 500g unsweetened chocolate chips

1. Preheat the oven to 170°C (150°C fan) and line a baking tray with parchment paper.
2. In a large mixing bowl, cream together the butter and Swerve with a hand mixer on medium speed for about 3 minutes, or until light and fluffy. Add the eggs one at a time, scraping the sides as you go. Mix in the almond flour at low speed until combined.
3. Fold in the chocolate chips. Scoop 3 tablespoons of dough for each cookie, spacing them well apart on the tray. Bake for 15 minutes, or until golden and slightly crisp. Cool before serving.

Per Serving

Calories: **317** | Fat: **27g** | Carbs: **8.9g** | Protein: **6.3g**

RUM BROWNIES

Prep time: **5 minutes** | Cook time: **30 minutes** | Serves **8**

- 165g almond flour
- 125g coconut flour
- 5g baking powder
- 250g xylitol
- 125g unsweetened cocoa powder
- 2 eggs
- 170g butter, melted
- 85g unsweetened baking chocolate, melted
- 2 tbsp rum
- A pinch of salt
- A pinch of freshly grated nutmeg
- 1g ground cinnamon

1. In a mixing bowl, combine all the dry ingredients. In another bowl, mix together all the wet ingredients until well combined.
2. Stir the dry mixture into the wet ingredients, then spread evenly into a parchment-lined baking dish.
3. Bake in a preheated oven at 180°C (160°C fan) for 20 to 22 minutes, or until set. Cut into squares and serve.

Per Serving

Calories: **320** | Fat: **30.2g** | Carbs: **6.3g** | Protein: **5.9g**

CHAPTER 4

CAULIFLOWER SALAD WITH SHRIMP AND CUCUMBER

Prep time: 30 minutes | **Cook time: 15 minutes** | **Serves 6**

- 1 cauliflower head, florets only
- 450g medium shrimp
- 65g + 14ml olive oil, divided
- 2 cucumbers, peeled and chopped
- 42g fresh dill, chopped
- 65ml lemon juice
- 28g lemon zest

1. Heat 14ml olive oil in a skillet over medium heat and cook the shrimp until opaque, about 8-10 minutes.
2. Place the cauliflower florets in a microwave-safe bowl and microwave for 5 minutes. Combine the shrimp, cauliflower, and cucumber in a large bowl.
3. In a separate bowl, whisk together the remaining olive oil, lemon zest, lemon juice, dill, and a pinch of salt and pepper. Pour over the salad and toss to combine. Serve.

Per Serving

Calories: 214 | **Carbs: 5g** | **Fat: 17g** | **Protein: 15g**

STUFFED MINI PEPPERS

Prep time: 5 minutes | **Cook time: 25 minutes** | **Serves 6**

- 340g ground beef
- 125g onion, chopped
- 2 garlic cloves, minced
- 12 mini peppers, deseeded
- 125g cheddar cheese, grated

1. Heat a lightly oiled sauté pan over medium heat. Brown the ground beef for 3-4 minutes, stirring to break up any large chunks.
2. Add the onions and garlic and cook for another 2 minutes until softened and fragrant.
3. In a pot of boiling water, cook the peppers until just tender, about 7 minutes.
4. Place the peppers on a lined baking tray. Stuff each pepper with the beef mixture, then top with the grated cheddar cheese.
5. Bake at 180°C for approximately 17 minutes. Serve at room temperature.

Per Serving

Calories: 207 | **Fat: 10.2g** | **Carbs: 6.8g** | **Protein: 19.7g**

TWO CHEESE AND PROSCIUTTO BALLS

Prep time: 5 minutes | **Cook time: 10 minutes** | **Serves 4**

- 60g goat cheese, crumbled
- 60g feta cheese, crumbled
- 85g prosciutto, chopped
- 1 red pepper, deseeded and finely chopped
- 2 tablespoons sesame seeds, toasted

1. In a bowl, thoroughly combine the cheeses, prosciutto, and red pepper. Shape the mixture into small balls.
2. Place the balls on a platter and chill in the fridge until ready to serve.
3. Roll each cheese ball in toasted sesame seeds before serving.

Per Serving

Calories: 176 | **Fat: 12.9g** | **Carbs: 2.3g** | **Protein: 12.8g**

SNACKS AND APPETIZERS

CHOCOLATE PEANUT TRUFFLES

Prep time: **5 minutes** | Cook time: **1 hour 5 minutes** | Serves **6**

- 125ml coconut oil
- 125g no-added-sugar peanut butter
- 65g cocoa powder, unsweetened
- 65g xylitol
- 4 tbsp roasted peanuts, finely ground

1. Gently melt the coconut oil in the microwave, then stir in the peanut butter until well combined.
2. Mix in the cocoa powder and xylitol. Freeze for about 1 hour until firm enough to handle.
3. Shape into small balls and roll in the ground peanuts. Keep chilled until serving.

Per Serving

Calories: **328** | Fat: **32.6g** | Carbs: **7.7g** | Protein: **6.9g**

COCKTAIL MEATBALLS WITH CHEESE

Prep time: **5 minutes** | Cook time: **25 minutes** | Serves **10**

- 225g ground turkey
- 450g ground beef
- 4 ounces pork rinds, crushed
- 65ml full-fat milk
- 1 shallot, chopped
- 2 garlic cloves, minced
- Sea salt and black pepper, to taste
- 125g Romano cheese, grated

1. In a mixing bowl, combine all the ingredients and mix well. Shape the mixture into bite-sized meatballs.
2. Place the meatballs on a parchment-lined baking sheet and brush with olive oil.
3. Bake at 180°C for 10 minutes. Rotate the pan and bake for another 10 minutes. Serve with cocktail sticks and enjoy!

Per Serving

Calories: **247** | Fat: **18g** | Carbs: **1.1g** | Protein: **19.1g**

CLASSIC HOT CHICKEN DRUMETTES

Prep time: **5 minutes** | Cook time: **25 minutes** | Serves **6**

- 900g chicken drumettes
- Sea salt and black pepper, to taste
- 1g paprika
- 5g cayenne pepper
- 5g dried oregano
- 80g hot sauce
- 14g stone-ground mustard
- 5g garlic powder

1. Pat the drumettes dry with kitchen paper. Season with salt, black pepper, paprika, cayenne pepper, and oregano.
2. Brush the drumettes with a little oil and place them in a roasting pan. Bake at 210°C for 18 minutes.
3. Toss the cooked drumettes with the hot sauce, mustard, and garlic powder, then broil for 5 minutes more, or until golden brown. Serve warm.

Per Serving

Calories: **179** | Fat: **2.5g** | Carbs: **2.3g** | Protein: **34.2g**

CHAPTER 5: POULTRY

POULTRY

BUFFALO CHICKEN

Prep time: **10 minutes** | Cook time: **6 hours** | Serves **4**

- 3 tablespoons olive oil, divided
- 450g boneless chicken breasts
- 250g hot sauce
- ½ sweet onion, finely chopped
- 85ml coconut oil, melted
- 65ml water
- 5g minced garlic
- 2 tablespoons chopped fresh parsley, for garnish

1. Lightly grease the insert of the slow cooker with 14g of the olive oil.
2. In a large skillet over medium-high heat, heat the remaining 2 tablespoons of the olive oil. Add the chicken and brown for 5 minutes, turning once.
3. Transfer the chicken to the insert and arrange in one layer on the bottom.
4. In a small bowl, whisk together the hot sauce, onion, coconut oil, water, and garlic. Pour the mixture over the chicken.
5. Cover and cook on low for 6 hours.
6. Serve topped with the parsley.

Per Serving:

Calories: **376** | Fat: **31g** | Protein: **26g** | Carbs: **2g**

HUNGARIAN CHICKEN

Prep time: **10 minutes** | Cook time: **7 to 8 hours** | Serves **4**

- 14ml extra-virgin olive oil
- 900g boneless chicken thighs
- 125g chicken broth
- juice and zest of 1 lemon
- 10g minced garlic
- 10g paprika
- 1g salt
- 250g sour cream
- 14g chopped parsley, for garnish

1. Lightly grease the insert of the slow cooker with the olive oil.
2. Place the chicken thighs in the insert.
3. In a small bowl, stir together the broth, lemon juice and zest, garlic, paprika, and salt. Pour the broth mixture over the chicken.
4. Cover and cook on low for 7 to 8 hours.
5. Turn off the heat and stir in the sour cream.
6. Serve topped with the parsley.

Per Serving

Calories: **404** | Fat: **32g** | Protein: **23g** | Carbs: **4g**

ASIAN-STYLE TURKEY SOUP

Prep time: **5 minutes** | Cook time: **20 minutes** | Serves **5**

- 2 tablespoons canola oil
- 2 Oriental sweet peppers, deseeded and chopped
- 1 Bird's eye chilli, deseeded and chopped
- 2 spring onions, chopped
- 2.25L vegetable broth
- 450g turkey thighs, deboned and halved
- 1/10g five-spice powder
- 5g oyster sauce
- Kosher salt, to taste

1. Heat the canola oil in a stockpot over a moderate flame. Sauté the peppers and spring onions until softened, about 4 minutes.
2. Add the remaining ingredients and bring to a boil. Turn the heat to simmer, cover, and continue to cook for an additional 12 minutes.
3. Ladle into individual bowls and serve warm. Enjoy!

Per Serving

Calories: **180** | Fat: **7.5g** | Carbs: **6.7g** | Protein: **21.4g**

CHAPTER 5

TANGY CLASSIC CHICKEN DRUMETTES

Prep time: **5 minutes** | Cook time: **40 minutes** | Serves **4**

- 450g chicken drumettes
- 14ml olive oil
- 2 tablespoons butter, melted
- 1 garlic clove, sliced
- Fresh juice of ½ lemon
- 2 tablespoons white wine
- Salt and ground black pepper, to taste
- 14g fresh scallions, chopped

1. Preheat your oven to 220°C. Place the chicken in a parchment-lined baking tray. Drizzle with olive oil and melted butter.
2. Add the garlic, lemon juice, white wine, salt, and black pepper.
3. Bake in the preheated oven for about 35 minutes. Serve garnished with fresh scallions. Enjoy!

Per Serving

Calories: **209** | Fat: **12.2g** | Carbs: **0.4g** | Protein: **23.2g**

EASY TURKEY CURRY

Prep time: **5 minutes** | Cook time: **1 hour** | Serves **4**

- 15g sesame oil
- 450g boneless turkey wings, chopped
- 2 cloves garlic, finely chopped
- 1 small red chilli pepper, minced
- 1/10g turmeric powder
- 1/10g ginger powder
- 5g red curry paste
- 250g unsweetened coconut milk, preferably homemade
- 125ml water
- 125g turkey consommé
- Kosher salt and ground black pepper, to taste

1. Heat sesame oil in a sauté pan. Add the turkey and cook until it is light brown about 7 minutes.
2. Add garlic, chili pepper, turmeric powder, ginger powder, and curry paste and cook for 3 minutes longer.
3. Add the milk, water, and consommé. Season with salt and black pepper. Cook for 45 minutes over medium heat. Bon appétit!

Per Serving

Calories: **295** | Fat: **19.5g** | Carbs: **2.9g** | Protein: **25.5g**

CHEESY TURKEY BASE PIZZA WITH BACON

Prep time: **5 minutes** | Cook time: **35 minutes** | Serves **4**

- 225g minced turkey
- 125g Parmesan cheese, freshly grated
- 125g Mozzarella cheese, grated
- Salt and freshly ground black pepper, to taste
- 1 pepper (any colour), sliced
- 2 slices back bacon, roughly chopped
- 1 tomato, diced
- 5g dried oregano
- 2g dried basil

1. Preheat the oven to 180°C (160°C fan/gas mark 4).
2. In a mixing bowl, thoroughly combine the minced turkey, cheeses, salt, and black pepper.
3. Press the turkey-cheese mixture onto a baking tray lined with greaseproof paper. Bake for 22 minutes.
4. Top with pepper, bacon, tomato, oregano, and basil. Bake for a further 10 minutes until golden.
5. Serve hot.

Per Serving

Calories: **360** | Fat: **22.7g** | Carbs: **5.9g** | Protein: **32.6g**

POULTRY

CHEESY RANCH CHICKEN

Prep time: **5 minutes** | Cook time: **20 minutes** | Serves **4**

- 2 chicken breasts
- 30g butter, melted
- 5g salt
- 2g garlic granules
- 2g cayenne pepper
- 2g black peppercorns, crushed
- 7g ranch seasoning mix
- 115g ricotta cheese, at room temperature
- 125g Monterey Jack cheese, grated
- 4 rashers streaky bacon, chopped
- 65g spring onions, finely sliced

1. Preheat the oven to 185°C (165°C fan/gas mark 5).
2. Brush the chicken with melted butter. Season with salt, garlic granules, cayenne pepper, black pepper, and ranch seasoning mix.
3. Heat a heavy-based frying pan over medium heat. Cook the chicken for 3-5 minutes on each side until golden.
4. Transfer the chicken to a lightly greased ovenproof dish.
5. Top with both cheeses and bacon. Bake for about 12 minutes until the cheese is bubbling.
6. Scatter with spring onions before serving.

Per Serving

Calories: **295** | Fat: **19.5g** | Carbs: **2.9g** | Protein: **25.5g**

CHICKEN & SQUASH TRAYBAKE

Prep time: **60 minutes** | Cook time: **45 minutes** | Serves **4**

- 900g chicken thighs
- 450g butternut squash, cut into 3cm cubes
- 125g black olives, pitted
- 65ml olive oil
- 5 garlic cloves, thinly sliced
- 15g dried oregano
- Salt and freshly ground black pepper, to taste

1. Preheat the oven to 200°C (180°C fan/gas mark 6).
2. Lightly oil a large roasting tin.
3. Place the chicken thighs skin-side down in the tin.
4. Scatter the garlic, olives, and butternut squash around the chicken.
5. Drizzle everything with the remaining oil.
6. Season well with salt, pepper, and oregano.
7. Roast for 45 minutes, turning the chicken skin-side up halfway through, until golden and cooked through.

Per Serving

Calories: **411** | Fat: **15g** | Carbs: **5.5g** | Protein: **31g**

SPICY CHEESE CHICKEN SOUP

Prep time: **15 minutes** | Cook time: **5 minutes** | Serves **4**

- 125g green enchilada sauce
- 500g cooked chicken, shredded
- 500ml chicken stock
- 250g mature Cheddar cheese, grated
- 115g cream cheese
- 3g chilli powder
- 3g ground cumin
- 3g fresh basil, chopped
- Salt and freshly ground black pepper, to taste

1. In a food processor, blend the cream cheese, enchilada sauce, and stock until smooth.
2. Pour into a large saucepan over medium heat. Heat through but do not boil.
3. Add the chicken, chilli powder, and cumin. Cook for 3-5 minutes until piping hot.
4. Stir in the Cheddar cheese until melted. Season with salt and pepper.
5. Serve hot, garnished with fresh basil.

Per Serving

Calories: **346** | Carbs: **3g** | Fat: **23g** | Protein: **25g**

CHAPTER 5

SPICED CHICKEN KEBABS WITH TAHINI SAUCE

Prep time: **20 minutes** | Cook time: **10 minutes** | Serves **4**

- 42ml soy sauce
- 14g ginger-garlic paste
- 28g brown sugar alternative
- 28ml olive oil
- 3 chicken breasts, cut into 3cm chunks
- 125g tahini
- 3g garlic granules
- Salt and chilli flakes to taste

1. In a bowl, whisk together soy sauce, ginger-garlic paste, sugar alternative, chilli flakes, and olive oil.
2. Place the chicken in a zip-lock bag, add the marinade, seal, and shake to coat evenly. Marinate in the fridge for 2 hours.
3. Preheat the barbecue or grill to high (200°C).
4. Thread the chicken onto metal skewers or wooden skewers that have been soaked in water.
5. Cook for about 10 minutes, turning 3-4 times until golden brown and cooked through.
6. Meanwhile, mix the tahini, garlic granules, salt, and 65ml warm water to make the sauce.
7. Serve the kebabs with the tahini sauce and cauliflower rice, if desired.

Per Serving

Calories: **225** | Carbs: **2g** | Fat: **17.4g** | Protein: **15g**

LEMON CHICKEN KEBABS

Prep time: **2 hours 17 minutes** | Cook time: **5 minutes** | Serves **4**

- 3 chicken breasts, cut into 3cm chunks
- 28ml olive oil, divided
- ⅔ jar preserved lemons, flesh removed, rind only
- 2 garlic cloves, finely chopped
- 125ml lemon juice
- Salt and freshly ground black pepper to taste
- 5g fresh rosemary leaves, to garnish
- 2-4 lemon wedges, to serve

1. Thread the chicken pieces onto metal skewers or wooden skewers that have been soaked in water.
2. In a large shallow dish, mix half the oil with the garlic, salt, pepper, lemon juice, and preserved lemon rind.
3. Add the chicken skewers, cover, and marinate in the fridge for at least 2 hours.
4. When ready to cook, preheat the grill to high (170°C).
5. Cook the skewers for 6 minutes on each side until golden brown and cooked through.
6. Serve hot, garnished with rosemary leaves and lemon wedges.

Per Serving

Calories: **350** | Fat: **11g** | Carbs: **3.5g** | Protein: **34g**

KETO TURKEY LETTUCE WRAPS

Prep time: **5 minutes** | Cook time: **10 minutes** | Serves **4**

- 125g mayonnaise
- 5g dried basil
- 3g sea salt
- 1g freshly ground black pepper
- 8 cos lettuce leaves
- 450g sliced turkey breast
- 8 rashers turkey bacon, cooked
- 2 plum tomatoes, sliced

1. Mix the mayonnaise, basil, salt, and pepper in a small bowl.
2. Spread the mayonnaise mixture evenly inside each lettuce leaf.
3. Fill each leaf with equal portions of turkey breast, bacon, and tomatoes.
4. Serve immediately.

Per Serving

Calories: **271** | Fat: **14g** | Protein: **26g** | Carbs: **7.6g**

POULTRY

ROASTED STUFFED CHICKEN WITH TOMATO BASIL SAUCE

Prep time: **35 minutes** | Cook time: **5 minutes** | Serves **6**

- 115g cream cheese
- 85g mozzarella slices
- 280g fresh spinach
- 85g mozzarella, grated
- 15ml olive oil
- 250g tomato and basil sauce
- 3 large chicken breasts

1. Preheat the oven to 200°C (180°C fan/gas mark 6).
2. Place the cream cheese, grated mozzarella, and spinach in a microwave-safe bowl. Heat in short bursts until the cheese begins to melt, then stir to combine.
3. Make deep horizontal cuts in each chicken breast to create a pocket.
4. Fill each pocket with the spinach mixture.
5. Brush the chicken with olive oil and place in a lined baking dish.
6. Bake for 25 minutes.
7. Pour over the tomato sauce and top with mozzarella slices.
8. Return to the oven for 5 minutes until the cheese is bubbling.

Per Serving

Calories: **338** | Fat: **28g** | Carbs: **2.5g** | Protein: **37g**

SPICY CHICKEN KABOBS

Prep time: **20 minutes + marinade time** | Serves **6**

- 900g chicken breasts, cut into 3cm chunks
- 5ml sesame oil
- 15ml olive oil
- 250g red pepper, cut into chunks
- 28g Chinese five-spice powder
- 28g granulated sweetener
- 15ml fish sauce

1. Mix the sesame oil, olive oil, fish sauce, and seasonings in a bowl.
2. Add the chicken, cover, and marinate in the fridge for 1 hour.
3. Preheat the grill to high.
4. Thread the chicken and peppers alternately onto 12 metal skewers (or wooden skewers that have been soaked in water).
5. Grill for 3 minutes on each side until golden brown and cooked through.

Per Serving

Calories: **198** | Fat: **13.5g** | Carbs: **3.1g** | Protein: **17.5g**

CRISPY CHEDDAR-COATED CHICKEN

Prep time: **40 minutes** | Cook time: **37 minutes** | Serves **4**

- 2 large eggs
- 45g butter, melted
- 750g mature Cheddar cheese, coarsely grated
- 125g pork scratchings, finely crushed
- 450g chicken mini fillets
- Pink Himalayan salt, to season
- Sweet mustard dip, to serve (optional)

1. Preheat the oven to 175°C (155°C fan/gas mark 4). Line a baking tray with greaseproof paper.
2. Whisk together the eggs and melted butter in a shallow bowl.
3. In another bowl, combine the grated Cheddar and crushed pork scratchings.
4. Season the chicken with salt, then dip each piece in the egg mixture, followed by the cheese mixture, pressing to coat well.
5. Arrange on the prepared baking tray, cover with foil, and bake for 25 minutes.
6. Remove the foil and cook for a further 12 minutes until golden brown and crispy.
7. Serve with sweet mustard dip and vegetable fries, if desired.

Per Serving

Calories: **203** | Carbs: **3g** | Fat: **14g** | Protein: **12g**

39

CHAPTER 5

COURGETTI WITH TURKEY RAGU

Prep time: **30 minutes** | Cook time: **30 minutes** | Serves **6**

- 500g mushrooms, sliced
- 10ml olive oil
- 450g minced turkey
- 40g basil pesto
- 250g onion, diced
- 500g broccoli florets
- 1.5kg courgettes, spiralized

1. Heat the oil in a large frying pan. Add the spiralized courgettes and cook for 2-3 minutes, stirring frequently. Remove and set aside.
2. In the same pan, brown the turkey for 7-8 minutes. Transfer to a plate.
3. Add the onion to the pan and cook until softened, about 3 minutes.
4. Add the broccoli and mushrooms, cooking for 7 minutes more.
5. Return the turkey to the pan and stir in the pesto.
6. Cover, reduce heat, and simmer for 15 minutes.
7. Stir through the courgetti and serve immediately.

Per Serving

Calories: **273** | Fat: **16g** | Carbs: **3.8g** | Protein: **19g**

GRILLED BOK CHOY CAESAR SALAD WITH CHICKEN

Prep time: **1 hour 20 minutes** | Cook time: **10 minutes** | Serves **4**

- For the chicken:
- 4 chicken thighs
- 65ml lemon juice
- 2 garlic cloves, finely chopped
- 30ml olive oil
- For the salad:
- 125ml Caesar dressing
- 30ml olive oil
- 12 bok choy leaves
- 3 Parmesan crisps
- Parmesan cheese, freshly grated, to serve

1. Place the chicken ingredients in a food bag. Seal, shake to combine, and refrigerate for 1 hour.
2. Preheat the grill to medium-high.
3. Grill the chicken for about 4 minutes each side until cooked through.
4. Slice the bok choy leaves lengthways and brush with oil.
5. Grill for about 3 minutes until lightly charred.
6. Arrange on a serving platter, top with the chicken, and drizzle with Caesar dressing.
7. Finish with grated Parmesan and the Parmesan crisps.

Per Serving

Calories: **529** | Carbs: **5g** | Fat: **39g** | Protein: **33g**

CREAMY SPINACH CHICKEN

Prep time: **35 minutes** | Cook time: **15 minutes** | Serves **4**

- 450g chicken thighs
- 30ml coconut oil
- 30g coconut flour
- 500g fresh spinach, roughly chopped
- 5g dried oregano
- 250ml double cream
- 250ml chicken stock
- 30g butter

1. Heat the coconut oil in a large frying pan and brown the chicken on all sides for 6-8 minutes. Remove and set aside.
2. In the same pan, melt the butter and whisk in the flour over medium heat.
3. Gradually whisk in the cream and stock, bringing to the boil. Stir in the oregano.
4. Add the spinach and cook until wilted.
5. Return the chicken to the pan and cook for a further 15 minutes until thoroughly cooked.

Per Serving

Calories: **446** | Fat: **38g** | Carbs: **2.6g** | Protein: **18g**

POULTRY

ROAST CHICKEN WITH BRUSSELS SPROUTS

Prep time: **120 minutes** | Cook time: **55 minutes** | Serves **8**

- 2.2kg whole chicken
- 1 bunch fresh oregano
- 1 bunch fresh thyme
- 15g fresh marjoram
- 15g fresh parsley
- 15ml olive oil
- 900g Brussels sprouts, trimmed
- 1 lemon
- 60g butter, softened

1. Preheat the oven to 225°C (205°C fan/gas mark 7).
2. Stuff the chicken cavity with oregano, thyme, and the lemon, halved.
3. Tuck the wing tips under the body.
4. Roast for 15 minutes.
5. Reduce heat to 160°C (140°C fan/gas mark 3) and cook for 40 minutes.
6. Spread butter over the chicken and sprinkle with parsley and marjoram.
7. Add the Brussels sprouts around the chicken.
8. Return to oven for 40 minutes until chicken is golden and cooked through.
9. Rest for 10 minutes before carving.

Per Serving

Calories:**430** | Carbs:**5g** | Fat: **32g** | Protein: **30g**

HERBED BUTTER CHICKEN LEGS

Prep time: **5 minutes** | Cook time: **20 minutes** | Serves **4**

- 30g butter, softened
- 5 chicken legs, skinless
- 2 spring onions, finely chopped
- 5g fresh basil, chopped
- 5g fresh thyme, chopped
- 1 garlic clove, finely chopped
- 2g black peppercorns, freshly cracked
- 250ml vegetable stock
- 2g paprika
- Sea salt, to taste

1. Melt 15g butter in a large frying pan over medium-high heat.
2. Brown the chicken legs for 4-5 minutes each side.
3. Add spring onions, basil, thyme, and garlic; sauté for 1 minute.
4. Add remaining butter, peppercorns, stock, and paprika.
5. Bring to the boil, then reduce to a simmer.
6. Cook for 10 minutes until chicken is cooked through.
7. Season with salt and serve.

Per Serving

Calories: **370** | Fat: **16g** | Carbs: **0.9g** | Protein: **51g** | Fiber: **0.2g**

ASIAN-GLAZED CHICKEN LEGS

Prep time: **5 minutes** | Cook time: **25 minutes** | Serves **4**

- 15ml sesame oil
- 4 chicken legs
- 65ml Shaoxing rice wine
- 2 tablespoons brown sugar substitute
- 65g chilli sauce

1. Heat the sesame oil in a heavy-based frying pan over medium-high heat. Sear the chicken legs until golden on all sides; set aside.
2. Add a splash of rice wine to the same pan to deglaze.
3. Pour in the remaining wine, sugar substitute and chilli sauce. Bring to the boil, then immediately reduce the heat to medium-low.
4. Simmer for 5-10 minutes until the sauce coats the back of a spoon. Return the chicken legs to the pan.
5. Cook for a further 3 minutes until the chicken is well coated and heated through.

Per Serving

Calories: **367** | Fat: **14.7g** | Carbs: **3.5g** | Protein: **51.2g**

CHAPTER 5

CITRUS BEER-GLAZED CHICKEN WINGS

Prep time: **30 minutes** | Cook time: **10 minutes** | Serves **4**

- 250ml gluten-free beer
- Pinch of garlic granules
- 5g grapefruit zest
- 45ml lemon juice
- 3g ground coriander
- 15ml fish sauce
- 30g butter
- 1g xanthan gum
- 40g low-carb sweetener
- 20 chicken wings
- Salt and freshly ground black pepper

1. In a saucepan, combine lemon juice, zest, fish sauce, coriander, beer, sweetener, and garlic.
2. Bring to the boil, cover, reduce heat, and simmer for 10 minutes.
3. Stir in butter and xanthan gum until sauce thickens. Set aside.
4. Season wings with salt and pepper.
5. Preheat grill to high.
6. Grill wings for 5 minutes each side until cooked through.
7. Serve topped with the citrus sauce.

Per Serving

Calories: **365** | Carbs: **4g** | Fat: **25g** | Protein: **21g**

CHICKEN AND SPINACH GRATIN

Prep time: **45 minutes** | Cook time: **35 minutes** | Serves **4**

- 6 chicken breasts
- 5g mixed herbs
- Salt and freshly ground black pepper
- 350g baby spinach
- 15ml olive oil
- 115g cream cheese, cubed
- 270g mozzarella, grated
- 60ml water

1. Preheat oven to 190°C (170°C fan/gas mark 5).
2. Season chicken with mixed herbs, salt, and pepper.
3. Place in an ovenproof dish and layer spinach over the chicken.
4. Mix oil with cream cheese, mozzarella, salt, and pepper.
5. Gradually stir in water until combined.
6. Pour over the chicken and cover with foil.
7. Bake for 20 minutes, then remove foil.
8. Cook for 15 minutes more until golden.
9. Rest for 5 minutes before serving with braised asparagus.

Per Serving

Calories: **340** | Carbs: **1g** | Fat: **30.2g** | Protein: **15g**

BAKED BUFFALO CHICKEN WINGS

Prep time: **5 minutes** | Cook time: **1 hour** | Serves **6**

- 15ml olive oil
- 900g chicken wings
- 125g butter, melted
- 125ml hot pepper sauce
- 2 tbsp white wine vinegar
- 1 tsp garlic granules
- Sea salt and freshly ground black pepper, to taste

1. Preheat the oven to 160°C/140°C fan/Gas mark 3. Brush a baking tray with olive oil. Arrange the chicken wings in a single layer.
2. Make the sauce by whisking together the melted butter, hot pepper sauce, white wine vinegar, garlic granules, salt and pepper until well combined.
3. Pour the sauce over the wings. Bake for 55 minutes, turning once or twice during cooking.
4. Check seasoning and serve hot.

Per Serving

Calories: **288** | Fat: **20.6g** | Carbs: **1.4g** | Protein: **23.5g**

POULTRY

ROSEMARY CHICKEN WITH AVOCADO SAUCE

Prep time: **22 minutes** | Cook time: **12 minutes** | Serves **4**

- 1 ripe avocado, stoned
- 125g mayonnaise
- 40g ghee
- 4 chicken breasts
- Salt and freshly ground black pepper
- 250g fresh rosemary, chopped
- 125ml chicken stock

1. Blend avocado, mayonnaise, and salt in a food processor until smooth.
2. Season to taste and refrigerate until needed.
3. Heat ghee in a large frying pan.
4. Season chicken with salt and pepper.
5. Fry for 4 minutes each side until golden.
6. Remove chicken to a plate.
7. Add stock and rosemary to pan.
8. Simmer for 3 minutes, then return chicken.
9. Cover and cook on low for 5 minutes until liquid reduces.
10. Serve chicken with avocado sauce, buttered green beans and baby carrots.

Per Serving

Calories: **398** | Carbs: **4g** | Fat: **32g** | Protein: **24g**

PESTO CHICKEN

Prep time: **5 minutes** | Cook time: **30 minutes** | Serves **4**

For the chicken:
- 2 tbsp vegetable oil
- 4 chicken breast escalopes

For the pesto:
- 500g fresh basil leaves
- 65ml extra virgin olive oil
- 65g pine nuts
- 65g coconut flour
- 1 tsp sea salt
- 1 garlic clove
- 2 tbsp freshly grated Parmesan (optional)

1. Heat the oil in a large frying pan over medium heat.
2. Coat each chicken escalope with coconut flour and place in the pan. Cook for 3-4 minutes on each side.
3. Meanwhile, make the pesto. Place the basil leaves, olive oil, pine nuts, salt and garlic in a food processor and blitz until smooth. Stir in the cheese, if using.
4. When the chicken is almost done, pour the pesto over and cook for 3-5 minutes, or until the chicken is cooked through and the internal temperature reaches 75°C.

Per Serving

Calories: **430** | Fat: **33.1g** | Protein: **13.2g** | Carbs: **20.1g**

CHICKEN PUTTANESCA

Prep time: **5 minutes** | Cook time: **25 minutes** | Serves **5**

- 30ml olive oil
- 1 pepper, chopped
- 1 red onion, chopped
- 2 cloves garlic, finely chopped
- 750g boneless chicken thighs
- 500g passata
- 15g capers
- 1 tsp dried chilli flakes
- 65g Parmesan cheese, freshly grated
- 2 sprigs fresh basil, chopped

1. Heat the olive oil in a non-stick frying pan over medium heat. Once hot, sauté the peppers and onions until tender and fragrant.
2. Add the garlic and cook for a further 30 seconds.
3. Stir in the chicken, passata, capers and chilli flakes; continue to cook for 20 minutes or until thoroughly heated.
4. Serve garnished with freshly grated Parmesan and basil.

Per Serving

Calories: **265** | Fat: **11.4g** | Carbs: **6.5g** | Protein: **32.5g**

CHAPTER 6: BEEF, LAMB AND PORK

BEEF, LAMB AND PORK

CLASSIC HOMEMADE BEEFBURGERS

Prep time: **5 minutes** | Cook time: **20 minutes** | Serves **6**

- 700g minced chuck steak
- 60g bacon, finely chopped
- 1 shallot, finely chopped
- 2 garlic cloves, crushed
- 4 tbsp ground almonds
- 2 tbsp ground flaxseed
- 1 tsp mustard seeds
- Sea salt and freshly ground black pepper
- 1 tsp smoked paprika

1. Mix all ingredients thoroughly in a large bowl. Shape into 6 equal patties.
2. Heat a lightly oiled griddle pan over medium-high heat. Cook the burgers for about 5 minutes each side.
3. Serve in low-carb burger buns.

Per Serving

Calories: **325** | Fat: **21.5g** | Carbs: **1.3g** | Protein: **29.9g**

BALSAMIC SLOW-COOKED BEEF

Prep time: **15 minutes** | Cook time: **7 to 8 hours** | Serves **8**

- 45ml extra virgin olive oil, divided
- 900g boneless beef chuck
- 250ml beef stock
- 125ml balsamic vinegar
- 15g garlic, crushed
- 15g granulated sweetener
- 1 tsp dried chilli flakes
- 15g fresh thyme, chopped

1. Lightly oil the slow cooker bowl with 15ml of olive oil.
2. Heat remaining oil in a large frying pan over medium-high heat. Brown the beef on all sides (about 7 minutes). Transfer to slow cooker.
3. Whisk together the stock, vinegar, garlic, sweetener, chilli flakes and thyme.
4. Pour the sauce over the beef.
5. Cover and cook on low for 7-8 hours.
6. Serve hot.

Per Serving:

Calories: **476** | Fat: **39g** | Protein: **28g** | Carbs: **1g**

PESTO SLOW-COOKED BEEF

Prep time: **5 minutes** | Cook time: **9 to 10 hours** | Serves **8**

- 15ml extra virgin olive oil
- 900g beef chuck
- 185g fresh pesto
- 125ml beef stock

1. Lightly oil the slow cooker bowl with olive oil.
2. Spread the pesto evenly over the beef. Place in the slow cooker and pour in the stock.
3. Cover and cook on low for 9-10 hours.
4. Serve hot.

Per Serving

Calories: **530** | Fat: **43g** | Protein: **32g** | Carbs: **2g**

CHAPTER 6

BBQ PULLED PORK PIZZA WITH GOAT'S CHEESE

Prep time: **30 minutes** | Cook time: **25 minutes** | Serves **4**

- 1 low-carb pizza base
- Olive oil for brushing
- 250g Manchego cheese, grated
- 500g leftover pulled pork
- 125ml sugar-free BBQ sauce
- 250g goat's cheese, crumbled

1. Preheat the oven to 200°C/180°C fan/Gas mark 6.
2. Place pizza base on a baking tray. Brush with olive oil and sprinkle with Manchego.
3. Mix pork with BBQ sauce and spread over the cheese.
4. Top with crumbled goat's cheese and bake for 25 minutes until cheese has melted.
5. Cut into slices and serve.

Per Serving

Calories:**344** | Fat: **24g** | Carbs: **6,5g** | Protein: **18g**

LOW-CARB PORK NACHOS

Prep time: **15 minutes** | Cook time: **10 minutes** | Serves **4**

- 1 pack low-carb tortilla chips
- 500g leftover pulled pork
- 1 red pepper, deseeded and chopped
- 1 red onion, diced
- 500g Monterey Jack cheese, grated

1. Preheat the oven to 170°C/150°C fan/Gas mark 3.
2. Layer the chips in a medium cast-iron pan, top with pork, peppers, and onion, then sprinkle with cheese.
3. Bake for 10 minutes until cheese has melted.
4. Let rest for 3 minutes before serving.

Per Serving

Calories:**452** | Fat: **25g** | Carbs: **9.3g** | Protein: **22g**

HERBED PORK CHOPS WITH RASPBERRY SAUCE

Prep time: **17 minutes** | Cook time: **5 minutes** | Serves **4**

For the pork:
- 15ml olive oil, plus extra for brushing
- 900g pork chops
- Pink salt and freshly ground black pepper

For the sauce:
- 500g raspberries
- 65ml water
- 20g mixed Italian herbs
- 45ml balsamic vinegar
- 10ml Worcestershire sauce

1. Heat oil in a frying pan over medium heat. Season pork with salt and pepper and cook for 5 minutes each side. Transfer to serving plates, reserving pan juices.
2. Mash raspberries in a bowl until jammy. Transfer to a saucepan with water and herbs. Simmer for 4 minutes.
3. Stir in reserved pan juices, vinegar, and Worcestershire sauce. Simmer for 1 minute.
4. Spoon sauce over pork chops and serve with braised broccoli rabe.

Per Serving

Calories:**413** | Fat: **32.5g** | Carbs: **1.1g** | Protein: **26.3g**

BEEF, LAMB AND PORK

BALSAMIC-MARINATED PORK CHOPS

Prep time: **2 hours 20 minutes** | Cook time: **10 minutes** | Serves **6**

- 6 boneless pork loin chops
- 30g sweetener
- 65ml balsamic vinegar
- 3 garlic cloves, crushed
- 65ml olive oil
- 5g salt
- Freshly ground black pepper

1. Place pork in a food bag. Mix sweetener, vinegar, garlic, oil, salt and pepper in a bowl, then pour over the pork. Seal bag and refrigerate for 2 hours.
2. Preheat the barbecue to medium heat.
3. Remove pork from marinade and grill covered for 10 minutes each side.
4. Rest for 4 minutes before serving with sautéed parsnips.

Per Serving

Calories: **418** | Fat: **26.8g** | Carbs: **1.5g** | Protein: **38.1g**

GARLIC STEAK BITES WITH COURGETTI

Prep time: **5 minutes** | Cook time: **45 minutes** | Serves **4**

- 450g sirloin steak
- 65ml coconut aminos
- 15ml hot sauce
- Juice of 1 lime
- 2 garlic cloves, crushed
- 15ml avocado oil
- 3 large courgettes, spiralized
- Fresh basil, to taste

1. Cut steak into bite-sized pieces.
2. Mix coconut aminos, hot sauce, lime juice and garlic. Add steak, coat well and marinate for 30 minutes.
3. Heat a large frying pan over medium-high heat with avocado oil. Cook meat in batches to avoid overcrowding.
4. Cook for 3-4 minutes, then turn and cook for 1-2 minutes until well seared. Remove to a plate.
5. Add courgetti to the pan and cook for 2-3 minutes until just softened.
6. Serve steak over courgetti.

Per Serving

Calories: **312** | Fat: **18.1g** | Protein: **24.9g** | Carbs: **12.8g**

PAPRIKA PORK CHOPS

Prep time: **25 minutes** | Cook time: **10 minutes** | Serves **4**

- 4 pork chops
- Salt and freshly ground black pepper
- 45g paprika
- 185g ground cumin
- 5g chilli powder

1. Mix paprika, black pepper, cumin, salt and chilli powder in a bowl.
2. Coat the pork chops thoroughly with the spice mixture.
3. Heat a griddle pan over medium heat, cook pork chops for 5 minutes each side.
4. Serve with steamed vegetables.

Per Serving

Calories: **349** | Fat: **18.5g** | Carbs: **4g** | Protein: **41.8g**

CHAPTER 6

PEANUT BUTTER PORK STIR-FRY

Prep time: **23 minutes** | Cook time: **10 minutes** | Serves **4**

- 20g ghee
- 900g pork loin, cut into strips
- Pink salt and chilli flakes, to taste
- 10g ginger-garlic paste
- 65ml chicken stock
- 70g smooth peanut butter
- 500g mixed stir-fry vegetables
- Cauliflower rice, to serve

1. Melt ghee in a wok. Season pork with salt, chilli and ginger-garlic paste.
2. Add pork to wok and cook for 6 minutes until no longer pink.
3. Blend peanut butter with a little stock until smooth. Add to pork and stir for 2 minutes.
4. Pour in remaining stock, cook for 4 minutes, then add vegetables.
5. Simmer for 5 minutes. Season to taste and serve with basil-flavoured cauliflower rice.

Per Serving

Calories: **571** | Fat: **49g** | Carbs: **1g** | Protein: **22.5g**

COURGETTE BOATS WITH SPICED BEEF

Prep time: **25 minutes** | Cook time: **18 minutes** | Serves **4**

- 4 large courgettes
- 30ml olive oil
- 700g minced beef
- 1 medium red onion, chopped
- 30g roasted red peppers, chopped
- Pink salt and freshly ground black pepper
- 250g mature Cheddar, grated

1. Preheat the oven to 175°C/155°C fan/Gas mark 4.
2. Trim courgettes and halve lengthways. Scoop out flesh to create boats, then chop the removed flesh.
3. Heat oil in a frying pan. Add beef, onion, peppers and courgette flesh. Season well.
4. Cook for 6 minutes, breaking up the meat, until browned.
5. Fill courgette boats with beef mixture and top with cheese.
6. Bake on a greased tray for 15 minutes until cheese melts and courgettes are tender.
7. Rest for 2 minutes before serving with mixed salad leaves.

Per Serving

Calories: **335** | Carbs: **7g** | Fat: **24g** | Protein: **18g**

SAUSAGE, TOMATO AND PESTO SALAD

Prep time: **15 minutes** | Cook time: **4 minutes** | Serves **8**

- 8 pork sausages, sliced
- 500g mixed cherry tomatoes, halved
- 1kg baby spinach
- 15ml olive oil
- 450g Monterey Jack cheese, cubed
- 30ml lemon juice
- 250g fresh basil pesto
- Salt and freshly ground black pepper

1. Heat oil in a frying pan and cook sausage slices for 4 minutes each side.
2. In a large bowl, combine spinach, cheese, tomatoes, pesto and lemon juice.
3. Season with salt and pepper, then add the cooked sausage and toss well.

Per Serving

Calories: **365** | Fat: **26g** | Carbs: **6.8g** | Protein: **18g**

BEEF, LAMB AND PORK

RICH BEEF RAGÙ

Prep time: **5 minutes** | Cook time: **25 minutes** | Serves **6**

- 700g minced beef
- 1 pepper, deseeded and chopped
- 1 celery stick, chopped
- 125g shallots, chopped
- 2 garlic cloves, finely chopped
- 2 vine tomatoes, puréed
- 500ml beef bone broth
- 15g dried Italian herbs

1. Brown beef in a large saucepan until cooked through (about 5 minutes), breaking up any lumps. Set aside.
2. In the same pan, sauté peppers, celery and shallots, adding a splash of broth if needed, until softened.
3. Add garlic and cook for 30-40 seconds.
4. Stir in puréed tomatoes, broth and herbs. Bring to the boil.
5. Return beef to pan, reduce heat and simmer for 15 minutes until sauce has reduced by half.

Per Serving

Calories: **349** | Fat: **21.8g** | Carbs: **4.9g** | Protein: **34g**

WARMING WINTER BEEF RAGÙ

Prep time: **5 minutes** | Cook time: **25 minutes** | Serves **5**

- 2 tbsp olive oil
- 700g skirt steak, cut into strips
- 1 large leek, finely sliced
- 2 garlic cloves, crushed
- 250ml beef stock
- Salt and freshly ground black pepper

1. Heat the olive oil in a large heavy-bottomed pan over a medium-high heat. Cook the skirt steak in two batches for 5-6 minutes until well browned. Set aside and keep warm.
2. In the same pan, add the leeks and garlic, sautéing in the meat juices for 1-2 minutes until softened.
3. Pour in the beef stock and bring to the boil, scraping any flavourful bits from the bottom of the pan.
4. Return the meat to the pan and reduce the heat to medium-low. Simmer for 10-15 minutes until the sauce has reduced and thickened slightly.
5. Season to taste with salt and pepper. Serve in warmed bowls.

Per Serving

Calories: **368** | Fat: **22.3g** | Carbs: **3.1g** | Protein: **36.8g**

HEARTY BEEF AND SPRING ONION SOUP

Prep time: **5 minutes** | Cook time: **45 minutes** | Serves **4**

- 7g lard
- 340g chuck steak, diced
- 125g spring onions, chopped
- 1L beef bone broth
- 1 celery stick, chopped

1. Melt lard in a large saucepan over medium-high heat. Brown meat in batches (5-6 minutes); set aside.
2. Sauté spring onions in the pan juices for 2 minutes until tender.
3. Deglaze pan with a splash of broth, then add remaining broth, celery and reserved beef.
4. Bring to the boil, then reduce heat, cover and simmer for 30-35 minutes.
5. Season to taste and serve hot.

Per Serving

Calories: **181** | Fat: **8.6g** | Carbs: **2.1g** | Protein: **23.2g**

CHAPTER 6

TRADITIONAL BEEF BOURGUIGNON

Prep time: **5 minutes** | Cook time: **1 hour 20 minutes** | Serves **5**

- 700g braising steak, cut into 4cm chunks
- 2 tbsp herbes de Provence
- 1 onion, roughly chopped
- 1 celery stick, chopped
- 250ml Burgundy wine (or good quality red wine)
- 750ml water
- Salt and freshly ground black pepper

1. Heat a large casserole dish over a medium-high heat. Brown the beef in batches until sealed on all sides.
2. Add a splash of wine to deglaze the pan, scraping up any caramelised bits.
3. Stir in the herbes de Provence, onion, and celery. Pour in the remaining wine and water, stirring to combine. Bring to the boil, then reduce heat to low.
4. Cover and simmer gently for 1 hour 10 minutes, or until the meat is tender.
5. Season to taste. Serve with cauliflower rice if desired.

Per Serving

Calories: **217** | Fat: **5.5g** | Carbs: **3.9g** | Protein: **30g**

KING-SIZE BURGERS

Prep time: **25 minutes** | Cook time: **18 minutes** | Serves **4**

- 1 tablespoon olive oil
- 450g minced beef
- 2 spring onions, chopped
- 1 garlic clove, finely minced
- 14g fresh thyme leaves
- 28g almond flour
- 280ml beef stock
- 7g fresh parsley, chopped
- 7g Worcestershire sauce

1. Grease a baking dish with olive oil. In a large mixing bowl, combine all ingredients except the parsley. Mix well with your hands, then form the mixture into two large patties and place on a lined baking tray.
2. Bake at 185°C for about 18 minutes, or until golden and slightly crisp. Sprinkle with fresh parsley before serving.

Per Serving

Calories: **363** | Fat: **26g** | Carbs: **3.1g** | Protein: **25.4g**

PERFECT SUNDAY ROAST BEEF

Prep time: **5 minutes** | Cook time: **3 hours 10 minutes** | Serves **5**

- 25g dripping or beef fat
- 2 leeks, sliced
- 2 celery sticks, chopped
- 2 red peppers, sliced
- 2 ripe tomatoes, blitzed to a purée
- 1.1kg beef chuck roast
- Sea salt and freshly ground black pepper
- 1 tsp garlic powder
- 1 sprig fresh thyme
- 1 sprig fresh rosemary

1. Preheat the oven to 165°C/145°C fan/Gas Mark 3. Melt the dripping in a large casserole dish over a medium-high heat. Sauté the leeks, celery, and peppers for about 4 minutes until softened.
2. Transfer the vegetables to a large roasting tin.
3. Add the tomato purée, place the beef on top, and season well with salt, pepper, and garlic powder. Tuck the herb sprigs alongside.
4. Roast for 3 hours, or until the meat is tender and easily pulls apart with a fork.
5. Remove from the oven, rest for 15 minutes, then slice and serve with the pan juices.

Per Serving

Calories: **359** | Fat: **16.4g** | Carbs: **5.1g** | Protein: **47.5g**

BEEF, LAMB AND PORK

SPICED BEEF AND VEGETABLE SOUP

Prep time: **5 minutes** | Cook time: **1 hour 10 minutes** | Serves **4**

- 1 tbsp vegetable oil
- 450g braising steak, diced
- 2 celery sticks, chopped
- 500g broccoli florets
- 1 red pepper, deseeded and chopped
- 250g passata
- 750ml vegetable stock
- Sea salt and freshly ground black pepper
- 1 packet taco seasoning
- 1 bay leaf
- 2 tbsp fresh chives, roughly chopped

1. Heat the oil in a large saucepan over a medium-high heat. Brown the beef for 4-5 minutes until sealed all over.
2. Add the celery, broccoli, pepper, passata, stock, seasoning, and bay leaf.
3. Reduce the heat and simmer, partially covered, for 1 hour until the meat is tender and the vegetables are cooked through.
4. Remove the bay leaf, check the seasoning, and serve garnished with fresh chives.

Per Serving

Calories: **219** | Fat: **8.7g** | Carbs: **5.2g** | Protein: **26.4g**

STUFFED FLANK STEAK PINWHEELS

Prep time: **40 minutes** | Cook time: **18 minutes** | Serves **6**

- 700g flank steak
- Salt and freshly ground black pepper
- 160g feta cheese, crumbled
- 100g baby spinach
- 1 green chilli, finely chopped
- 65g fresh basil leaves, chopped

1. Preheat the oven to 200°C/180°C fan/Gas Mark 6. Lightly oil a baking tray.
2. Place the steak between two sheets of cling film and gently bash with a rolling pin to an even thickness. Remove the cling film and season well.
3. Sprinkle half the feta over the steak, then layer with spinach, chilli, and basil. Top with the remaining feta.
4. Carefully roll up the steak, starting from a long edge, and secure with cocktail sticks at intervals.
5. Place on the prepared tray and roast for 15 minutes, turning once, until browned outside and the cheese has melted.
6. Rest for 3 minutes before slicing into pinwheels to serve.

Per Serving

Calories:**490** | Carbs:**2g** | Fat: **41g** | Protein: **28g**

CAULI RICE WITH VEGETABLES AND BEEF STEAK

Prep time: **25 minutes** | Cook time: **10 minutes** | Serves **4**

- 500g cauliflower rice
- 750g mixed vegetables
- 42g ghee
- 450g skirt steak
- Sea salt and freshly ground black pepper, to taste
- 4 fresh eggs
- Sugar-free hot sauce, for serving

1. In a bowl, combine the cauliflower rice with mixed vegetables. Sprinkle with a little water, then steam in the microwave for 1 minute until just tender. Divide between 4 serving bowls.
2. Melt the ghee in a frying pan over medium heat. Season the steak with salt and pepper, and sear for about 5 minutes on each side. Use a slotted spoon to add the beef to the vegetables.
3. Wipe the pan clean and crack an egg in, cooking until the white has set but the yolk is runny. Top each bowl with an egg and repeat for all servings. Drizzle with hot sauce before serving.

Per Serving

Calories: **320** | Carbs: **4g** | Fat: **26g** | Protein: **15g**

CHAPTER 6

MEAT AND GOAT CHEESE STUFFED MUSHROOMS

Prep time: 5 minutes | Cook time: 25 minutes | Serves 5

- 115g minced beef
- 55g minced pork
- Sea salt and freshly ground black pepper, to taste
- 65g goat's cheese, crumbled
- 2 tablespoons grated Romano cheese
- 2 tablespoons finely chopped shallot
- 1 garlic clove, finely minced
- 5g dried basil
- Pinch of dried oregano
- Pinch of dried rosemary
- 20 button mushrooms, stems removed

1. Combine all ingredients except the mushrooms in a large bowl. Spoon the mixture into each mushroom cap.
2. Preheat the oven to 190°C and bake the mushrooms for approximately 18 minutes or until golden. Serve warm or at room temperature.

Per Serving

Calories: 148 | Fat: 8.4g | Carbs: 4.8g | Protein: 14.1g

CAULIFLOWER CURRY WITH MINCED BEEF

Prep time: 25 minutes | Cook time: 21 minutes | Serves 6

- 1 tablespoon olive oil
- 680g minced beef
- 14g ginger and garlic paste
- 5g garam masala
- 200g canned whole tomatoes
- 1 small head of cauliflower, cut into florets
- Himalayan salt and ground chilli, to taste
- 65ml water

1. Heat the olive oil in a large saucepan over medium heat. Add the minced beef and ginger-garlic paste, then season with garam masala. Cook for 5 minutes, breaking up any lumps.
2. Stir in the tomatoes and cauliflower, seasoning with salt and chilli to taste. Cook for 6 minutes, then add the water and bring to a simmer. Allow it to reduce by half over the next 10 minutes.
3. Adjust seasoning if needed, and serve with konjac rice for a low-carb option.

Per Serving

Calories: 374 | Carbs: 2g | Fat: 33g | Protein: 22g

BUNLESS BEEF BURGERS WITH SRIRACHA

Prep time: 15 minutes | Cook time: 3 minutes | Serves 4

- 450g minced beef
- 3g onion powder
- 3g garlic powder
- 28g ghee
- 5g Dijon mustard
- Sea salt and freshly ground black pepper, to taste
- 4 keto buns (optional)
- 65g mayonnaise
- 5g sriracha
- 56g coleslaw

1. In a bowl, combine the minced beef, onion powder, garlic powder, Dijon mustard, salt, and pepper. Shape into 4 burger patties.
2. Heat the ghee in a large frying pan over medium heat. Cook the burgers for approximately 3 minutes on each side, or until done to your liking.
3. Serve each burger on a keto bun if desired, topped with mayonnaise, sriracha, and a spoonful of coleslaw.

Per Serving

Calories: 664 | Carbs: 7.9g | Fat: 55g | Protein: 39g

BEEF, LAMB AND PORK

CHEESE BEEF BURGERS WITH CAULI RICE CASSEROLE

Prep time: **30 minutes** | Cook time: **26 minutes** | Serves **6**

- 900g minced beef
- Sea salt and black pepper, to taste
- 250g cauliflower rice
- 500g cabbage, chopped
- 400g canned chopped tomatoes
- 65ml water
- 250g grated Colby Jack cheese

1. Preheat the oven to 190°C and lightly grease a baking dish.
2. In a pot, cook the minced beef with salt and pepper over medium heat until browned, about 6 minutes. Drain any excess fat, then add cauliflower rice, cabbage, tomatoes, and water. Cover and simmer for 5 minutes to thicken the mixture. Adjust the seasoning if needed.
3. Spoon the beef mixture into the prepared baking dish, top with grated cheese, and bake for 15 minutes until the cheese is melted and golden. Allow to cool for a few minutes before serving.

Per Serving

Calories: **335** | Carbs: **5g** | Fat: **25g** | Protein: **20g**

CREOLE BEEF TRIPE STEW

Prep time: **30 minutes** | Cook time: **12 minutes** | Serves **6**

- 680g beef tripe
- 1 litre buttermilk
- Sea salt, to taste
- 10g Creole seasoning
- 42ml olive oil, divided
- 2 large onions, sliced
- 3 tomatoes, diced

1. Place the tripe in a bowl and cover with buttermilk. Refrigerate for 3 hours to remove any strong flavour. Drain, pat dry with kitchen paper, and season with salt and Creole seasoning.
2. In a large frying pan, heat half the oil over medium heat. Brown the tripe on each side for a total of 6 minutes. Set aside.
3. Add the remaining oil to the pan, sauté the onions for 3 minutes, then add the tomatoes and cook for a further 10 minutes. Return the tripe to the pan, cover, and cook for an additional 3 minutes. Serve hot.

Per Serving

Calories: **342** | Carbs: **1g** | Fat: **27g** | Protein: **22g**

PORTOBELLO MUSHROOM BEEF BURGERS

Prep time: **15 minutes** | Cook time: **14 minutes** | Serves **4**

- 2 tbsp olive oil
- 450g lean minced beef
- 1 tbsp fresh parsley, finely chopped
- 1 tsp Worcestershire sauce
- Salt and freshly ground black pepper
- 2 slices mozzarella
- 2 large portobello mushroom caps
- Olive oil, for brushing

1. In a large bowl, combine the minced beef, parsley, Worcestershire sauce, salt and pepper. Mix thoroughly with clean hands, then shape into evenly-sized patties.
2. Preheat the grill to 200°C/180°C fan/Gas Mark 6. Brush the mushroom caps with olive oil and season with salt and pepper.
3. Place the mushroom caps gill-side up and the burger patties on the hot grill. Cook for 5 minutes, then turn the mushrooms and cook for another minute.
4. Place a slice of mozzarella on each patty. Continue cooking until the mushrooms are tender, about 4-5 minutes. Flip the patties and cook for 2-3 minutes until the cheese has melted.
5. Sandwich each patty between two mushroom caps and serve immediately.

Per Serving

Calories: **505** | Fat: **38.5g** | Carbs: **3.2g** | Protein: **38g**

53

CHAPTER 7: FISH AND SEAFOOD

FISH AND SEAFOOD

KETO WRAPS WITH ANCHOVIES

Prep time: **5 minutes** | Cook time: **10 minutes** | Serves **4**

- 2 x 57g tins anchovies in olive oil, drained
- 1 cucumber, sliced
- 500g red cabbage, shredded
- 1 red onion, finely chopped
- 5g Dijon mustard
- 4 tablespoons mayonnaise
- 1g freshly ground black pepper
- 1 large tomato, diced
- 12 large lettuce leaves

1. In a large mixing bowl, combine the anchovies with cucumber, cabbage, onion, mustard, mayonnaise, black pepper, and tomato.
2. Lay out the lettuce leaves on a tray. Spoon the anchovy and vegetable mixture onto each leaf, folding taco-style.
3. Repeat with remaining ingredients. Serve and enjoy!

Per Serving

Calories: **191** | Fat: **13.3g** | Carbs: **6.5g** | Protein: **9.9g**

HADDOCK FILLETS WITH MEDITERRANEAN SAUCE

Prep time: **5 minutes** | Cook time: **30 minutes** | Serves **4**

- 450g haddock fillets
- 1 tablespoon olive oil
- Sea salt and freshly cracked black pepper, to taste

For the Mediterranean Sauce:

- 2 spring onions, chopped
- A pinch of dried dill
- A pinch of dried oregano
- 5g fresh basil, chopped
- 65g mayonnaise
- 65g cream cheese, softened

1. Preheat the oven to 180°C. Drizzle the haddock fillets with olive oil and season with salt and black pepper.
2. Cover the fish with foil and bake for 20-25 minutes.
3. Meanwhile, prepare the sauce by mixing all ingredients in a bowl until smooth. Serve the warm haddock with the sauce on top.

Per Serving

Calories: **260** | Fat: **19.1g** | Carbs: **1.3g** | Protein: **19.6g**

COD WITH PARSLEY PISTOU

Prep time: **15 minutes** | Cook time: **10 minutes** | Serves **4**

- 250g fresh flat-leaf parsley, roughly chopped
- 1-2 small garlic cloves, finely minced
- Zest and juice of 1 lemon
- 5g sea salt
- 3g freshly ground black pepper
- 250ml extra-virgin olive oil, divided
- 450g cod fillets, cut into four portions

1. In a food processor, combine parsley, garlic, lemon zest and juice, salt, and pepper. Blend to chop.
2. with the processor running, gradually add 185ml olive oil until a thick consistency forms. Set aside.
3. In a skillet, heat the remaining olive oil over medium-high heat. Cook the cod fillets for 4-5 minutes on each side or until cooked through.
4. Stir the pistou into the pan to warm it, then coat the cod in the pistou. Serve warm.

Per Serving

Calories: **581** | Fat: **55g** | Carbs: **3g** | Protein: **21g**

CHAPTER 7

SHRIMP IN CREAMY PESTO OVER COURGETTI

Prep time: 10 minutes | Cook time: **10 minutes** | Serves **4**

- 450g fresh prawns, peeled and deveined
- Sea salt
- Freshly ground black pepper
- 2 tablespoons extra-virgin olive oil
- ½ small onion, thinly sliced
- 225g jarred pesto
- 185g crumbled goat's cheese or feta, plus extra for garnish
- 2 large courgettes, spiralised
- 65g flat-leaf parsley, chopped, for garnish

1. Season the prawns with salt and pepper.
2. In a large frying pan, heat olive oil over medium-high. Sauté the onion until lightly golden, about 5-6 minutes.
3. Lower the heat and add pesto and goat's cheese, stirring until the cheese melts. Simmer, then add the prawns and cover, cooking until pink, about 3-4 minutes.
4. Serve over courgetti, garnishing with parsley and extra cheese if desired.

Per Serving

Calories: **491** | Fat: **35g** | Carbs: **15g** | Protein: **29g**

SALMON WITH TARRAGON-DIJON SAUCE

Prep time: 5 minutes | Cook time: **15 minutes** | Serves **4**

- 600g salmon fillet (skin on or removed), cut into 4 pieces
- 65g avocado oil mayonnaise
- 65g Dijon mustard
- Zest and juice of ½ lemon
- 2 tablespoons fresh tarragon, chopped, or 1-2g dried
- 3g sea salt
- 1g freshly ground black pepper
- 4 tablespoons extra-virgin olive oil, for serving

1. Preheat the oven to 210°C. Line a baking tray with parchment paper.
2. Place salmon skin-side down on the tray.
3. In a small bowl, mix mayonnaise, mustard, lemon zest and juice, tarragon, salt, and pepper. Spread evenly on the salmon.
4. Bake for 10-12 minutes until lightly browned. Rest for 10 minutes on the tray. Drizzle with olive oil before serving.

Per Serving

Calories: **387** | Fat: **28g** | Carbs: **4g** | Protein: **29g**

GARLIC AND CHILLI PRAWNS

Prep time: 5 minutes | Cook time: **15 minutes** | Serves **5**

- 2 tablespoons butter
- 2 garlic cloves, minced
- 2 small dried cayenne chillies
- 900g prawns, peeled and deveined
- 65ml Manzanilla sherry
- Sea salt and freshly ground black pepper, to taste

1. Melt the butter in a pan over medium heat. Add garlic and cayenne chillies, cooking for 40 seconds.
2. Add the prawns and cook briefly, then add the sherry. Season with salt and black pepper.
3. Cook until the prawns are pink, about 2-3 minutes. Serve with lemon slices, if desired.

Per Serving

Calories: **203** | Fat: **5.5g** | Carbs: **1.8g** | Protein: **36.6g**

FISH AND SEAFOOD

SALT-AND-PEPPER SCALLOPS AND CALAMARI

Prep time: **5 minutes** | Cook time: **10 minutes** | Serves **4**

- 225g calamari steaks, sliced into strips or rings
- 225g sea scallops
- 7g sea salt, divided
- 5g freshly ground black pepper
- 5g garlic powder
- 85ml extra-virgin olive oil
- 28g butter

1. Place calamari and scallops on paper towels to drain. Sprinkle with 5g salt and leave to rest for 15 minutes.
2. Pat dry, then season with pepper and garlic powder.
3. In a frying pan, heat olive oil and butter on medium-high. Add seafood in a single layer, season with remaining salt, and cook for 2-4 minutes per side, until golden.
4. Remove from the pan with a slotted spoon, drizzle with the cooking oil, and serve.

Per Serving

Calories: **309** | Fat: **25g** | Carbs: **3g** | Protein: **18g**

MOM'S SEAFOOD CHOWDER

Prep time: **5 minutes** | Cook time: **30 minutes** | Serves **4**

- 2 tablespoons coconut oil
- 2 garlic cloves, crushed
- 1 shallot, chopped
- 250g broccoli florets
- 2 bell peppers, chopped
- 1 litre fish stock
- 4 tablespoons dry sherry
- 170g scallops
- 170g prawns, peeled and deveined
- 250ml double cream
- 2 tablespoons fresh chives, chopped

1. In a large pot, melt the coconut oil. Sauté the garlic and shallot for 3-4 minutes.
2. Add broccoli, bell peppers, and fish stock, bringing to a boil. Lower heat, partially cover, and simmer for 12 minutes.
3. Stir in sherry, scallops, prawns, and double cream, cooking for 7 minutes more.
4. Adjust seasoning and serve garnished with fresh chives. Enjoy!

Per Serving

Calories: **272** | Fat: **19.8g** | Carbs: **7g** | Protein: **16.6g**

LEMON AND HERB TILAPIA

Prep time: **30 minutes** | Cook time: **16 minutes** | Serves **4**

- 4 tilapia fillets
- 2 garlic cloves, minced
- 10g oregano
- 400g tinned diced tomatoes
- 1 tbsp olive oil
- ½ red onion, chopped
- 28g parsley
- 65g Kalamata olives

1. Heat the olive oil in a pan over medium heat, and cook the onion, garlic, and oregano for 3 minutes. Stir in tomatoes and bring to a simmer for 5 minutes.
2. Add olives and tilapia. Simmer for about 8 minutes. Serve topped with the tomato mixture.

Per Serving

Calories: **182** | Carbs: **6g** | Fat: **15g** | Protein: **23g**

CHAPTER 7

BASIL SHRIMP STEW WITH SRIRACHA SAUCE

Prep time: **25 minutes** | Cook time: **10 minutes** | Serves **6**

- 250ml coconut milk
- 28g lime juice
- 65g roasted peppers, diced
- 675g shrimp, peeled and deveined
- 65ml olive oil
- 1 garlic clove, minced
- 400g tinned diced tomatoes
- 28g sriracha sauce
- 65g onions, chopped
- 65g basil, chopped
- Fresh dill, chopped, for garnish
- Salt and black pepper, to taste

1. Heat the olive oil in a pot over medium heat. Add the onions and cook for 3 minutes, or until translucent. Add the garlic and cook for another minute.
2. Add tomatoes, shrimp, and basil. Simmer until shrimp turns opaque, about 3-4 minutes. Stir in sriracha and coconut milk, and simmer gently for 2 minutes (do not boil).
3. Stir in lime juice, season with salt and black pepper, and garnish with dill. Serve warm.

Per Serving

Calories: **324** | Carbs: **5g** | Fat: **21g** | Protein: **23g**

FISH CURRY MASALA

Prep time: **5 minutes** | Cook time: **25 minutes** | Serves **6**

- 2 tablespoons sesame oil
- 1 shallot, chopped
- 2 bell peppers, deveined and sliced
- 5g coriander, ground
- 5g cumin, ground
- 4 tablespoons red curry paste
- 5g ginger-garlic paste
- 675g white fish fillets, skinless and boneless
- 125g tomato sauce
- 125g bone broth
- 250ml coconut milk
- 10g red chilli powder
- Salt and black pepper, to taste

1. Heat the sesame oil in a saucepan over medium heat and sauté the shallot and bell peppers for 4 minutes, or until softened.
2. Stir in the coriander, cumin, curry paste, and ginger-garlic paste, cooking for an additional 4 minutes.
3. Add the fish, tomato sauce, bone broth, and coconut milk. Season with chilli powder, salt, and black pepper. Simmer for 5 minutes, or until fish is fully cooked. Serve warm.

Per Serving

Calories: **349** | Fat: **24.9g** | Carbs: **6.2g** | Protein: **22.7g**

LEMON CRAB CAKES

Prep time: **15 minutes** | Cook time: **3 minutes** | Serves **8**

- 2 tbsp coconut oil
- 1 tbsp lemon juice
- 250g lump crab meat
- 28g fresh parsley, chopped
- 10g Dijon mustard
- 1 egg, beaten
- 7g coconut flour

1. Place the crab meat in a bowl and add all other ingredients except the coconut oil. Mix well.
2. Form 8 small cakes from the mixture. Melt the coconut oil in a pan over medium heat and cook the crab cakes for 2-3 minutes per side, or until golden. Serve warm.

Per Serving

Calories: **65** | Carbs: **3.6g** | Fat: **5g** | Protein: **5.3g**

FISH AND SEAFOOD

TILAPIA CABBAGE TORTILLAS WITH CAULIFLOWER RICE

Prep time: 20 minutes | Cook time: **12 minutes** | Serves **4**

- 1 tsp avocado oil
- 250g cauliflower rice
- 4 tilapia fillets, cut into cubes
- 1g taco seasoning
- Sea salt and hot paprika, to taste
- 2 large cabbage leaves
- 28g guacamole
- 14g fresh basil, chopped

1. Microwave the cauliflower rice for 4 minutes in a microwave-safe bowl, fluff with a fork, and set aside.
2. Warm the avocado oil in a skillet over medium heat. Season the tilapia with taco seasoning, salt, and paprika. Cook for about 8 minutes, or until browned. Divide the fish among cabbage leaves and top with cauliflower rice, guacamole, and basil.

Per Serving

Calories:**170** | Fat: **6.4g** | Carbs:**1.4g** | Protein: **24.5g**

CRISPY SALMON WITH BROCCOLI & RED BELL PEPPER

Prep time: 30 minutes | Cook time: **22 minutes** | Serves **4**

- 4 salmon fillets
- Salt and black pepper, to taste
- 28g mayonnaise
- 28g crushed fennel seeds
- ½ head broccoli, cut into florets
- 1 red bell pepper, sliced
- 1 tbsp olive oil
- 2 lemon wedges, for garnish

1. Preheat the oven to 185°C. Brush the salmon with mayonnaise, season with salt and pepper, and coat with fennel seeds. Place on a lined baking sheet and bake for 15 minutes.
2. Steam the broccoli and red pepper for 3-4 minutes until tender. Sauté the red pepper in olive oil for 5 minutes, then add the broccoli and leave in the pan for 2-3 minutes. Serve with salmon, garnished with lemon wedges.

Per Serving

Calories:**563** | Fat: **37g** | Carbs:**6g** | Protein: **54g**

BLACKENED FISH TACOS WITH SLAW

Prep time: 20 minutes | Cook time: **5 minutes** | Serves **4**

- 1 tbsp olive oil
- 5g chilli powder
- 2 tilapia fillets
- 5g paprika
- 4 low-carb tortillas
- 125g red cabbage, shredded
- 1 tbsp lemon juice
- 1 tsp apple cider vinegar
- Salt and black pepper, to taste

1. Season the tilapia with chili powder and paprika. Heat the olive oil in a skillet over medium heat.
2. Add tilapia and cook until blackened, about 3 minutes per side. Cut into strips. Divide the tilapia between the tortillas. Combine all slaw ingredients in a bowl and top the fish to serve.

Per Serving

Calories:**268** | Fat: **20g** | Carbs: **3.5g** | Protein: **13.8g**

CHAPTER 7

CHILI COD WITH CHIVE SAUCE

Prep time: **20 minutes** | Cook time: **18 minutes** | Serves **4**

- 5g chilli powder
- 4 cod fillets
- Salt and black pepper, to taste
- 1 tbsp olive oil
- 1 garlic clove, minced
- 80ml lemon juice
- 28g vegetable stock
- 28g fresh chives, chopped

1. Preheat oven to 200 °C and grease a baking dish with cooking spray. Rub the cod fillets with chili powder, salt, and pepper and lay in the dish. Bake for 10-15 minutes.
2. In a skillet over low heat, warm olive oil and sauté garlic for 1 minute. Add lemon juice, vegetable stock, and chives. Season with salt, pepper, and cook for 3 minutes until the stock slightly reduces. Divide fish into 2 plates, top with sauce, and serve.

Per Serving

Calories: **448** | Fat: **35.3g** | Carbs: **6.3g** | Protein: **20g**

CRAB CAKES WITH COCONUT

Prep time: **15 minutes** | Cook time: **5 minutes** | Serves **8**

- 2 tbsp coconut oil
- 1 tbsp lemon juice
- 250g fresh white crab meat
- 1 tbsp Dijon mustard
- 1 medium egg, beaten
- 20g coconut flour
- Salt and freshly ground black pepper

1. In a large bowl, combine the crab meat, lemon juice, mustard, beaten egg, coconut flour, and seasoning. Mix gently to avoid breaking up the crab meat too much.
2. Shape the mixture into 8 even-sized patties.
3. Heat the coconut oil in a large frying pan over medium heat. Cook the crab cakes for 2-3 minutes on each side until golden brown and heated through.
4. Drain briefly on kitchen paper before serving.

Per Serving

Calories: **215** | Fat: **11.5g** | Carbs: **3.6g** | Protein: **15.3g**

HAND-ROLLED PRAWN SUSHI

Prep time: **10 minutes** | Cook time: **5 minutes** | Serves **5**

- 500g cooked prawns, roughly chopped
- 1 tbsp sriracha sauce
- ¼ cucumber, cut into thin strips
- 5 nori sheets
- 65g mayonnaise
- Reduced-salt soy sauce, to serve

1. In a bowl, mix together the prawns, mayonnaise, cucumber and sriracha sauce until well combined.
2. Lay a nori sheet on a clean work surface and spread about one-fifth of the prawn mixture along one edge.
3. Using the sushi mat if you have one, roll up tightly. Repeat with remaining ingredients.
4. Slice each roll into 6-8 pieces and serve with reduced-salt soy sauce.

Per Serving

Calories: **216** | Fat: **10g** | Carbs: **1g** | Protein: **18.7g**

FISH AND SEAFOOD

BAKED TROUT WITH ASPARAGUS

Prep time: **20 minutes** | Cook time: **15 minutes** | Serves **4**

- 450g asparagus spears, trimmed
- 2 tsp garlic purée
- 450g trout fillets, butterflied
- Salt and freshly ground black pepper
- 3 tbsp olive oil
- 2 sprigs fresh rosemary
- 2 sprigs fresh thyme
- 30g butter
- ½ red onion, thinly sliced
- 1 lemon, sliced

1. Preheat the oven to 200°C/180°C fan/Gas Mark 6. Rub the trout with garlic purée and season well.
2. Cut two large pieces of foil. Divide the fish between them and top each with equal portions of asparagus and onion.
3. Season the vegetables and add a sprig each of rosemary and thyme. Dot with butter and add lemon slices.
4. Wrap the foil to create sealed parcels and place on a baking tray. Bake for 15 minutes until the fish is cooked through.

Per Serving

Calories: **498** | Fat: **39.3g** | Carbs: **4.8g** | Protein: **27g**

TRADITIONAL FISH STEW

Prep time: **5 minutes** | Cook time: **30 minutes** | Serves **5**

- 1 tbsp beef dripping or oil
- 1 red onion, chopped
- 2 garlic cloves, crushed
- 1 green chilli, finely chopped
- Small bunch fresh dill, roughly chopped
- 1 ripe tomato, blitzed to a purée
- 250ml fish stock
- 500ml water
- 450g halibut, cut into chunks
- Sea salt and freshly ground black pepper
- ¼ tsp cayenne pepper
- ½ tsp curry powder
- 2 bay leaves

1. Melt the dripping in a large saucepan over medium-high heat. Gently cook the onion for 3 minutes, then add the garlic and chilli and cook for another minute.
2. Add the dill and tomato purée, cooking for 8 minutes more. Pour in the fish stock and water. Season with salt, pepper, cayenne, curry powder and bay leaves.
3. Reduce the heat and simmer for 15 minutes until well-flavoured. Add the halibut and cook until just done.
4. Check the seasoning and serve in warmed bowls.

Per Serving

Calories: **271** | Fat: **19.5g** | Carbs: **4.8g** | Protein: **18.5g**

SPICED FISH CAKES

Prep time: **5 minutes** | Cook time: **10 minutes** | Serves **5**

- 700g tilapia fillets, flaked
- 2 medium eggs, beaten
- 125g shallots, finely chopped
- 125g ground almonds
- 2 tbsp Cajun seasoning
- Oil for frying
- Little gem lettuce, to serve

1. In a large bowl, combine the flaked fish, beaten eggs, shallots, ground almonds and Cajun seasoning. Mix thoroughly.
2. Shape the mixture into 10 even-sized fish cakes. Chill in the refrigerator for 40 minutes to firm up.
3. Heat a little oil in a large frying pan over medium heat.
4. Cook the fish cakes for 3 minutes on each side until golden brown and heated through.
5. Drain briefly on kitchen paper and serve with lettuce leaves, if desired.

Per Serving

Calories: **238** | Fat: **10.9g** | Carbs: **2.6g** | Protein: **32.9g**

CHAPTER 7

MEDITERRANEAN-STYLE TILAPIA

Prep time: **30 minutes** | Cook time: **38 minutes** | Serves **4**

- 4 tilapia fillets
- 2 garlic cloves, finely chopped
- 1 tsp dried oregano
- 400g tin chopped tomatoes
- 1 tbsp olive oil
- ½ red onion, finely chopped
- Small bunch fresh parsley, chopped
- 65g pitted Kalamata olives

1. Heat the olive oil in a large frying pan over medium heat. Soften the onion for 3 minutes, then add the garlic and oregano and cook for another 30 seconds.
2. Add the tomatoes and bring to the boil. Reduce the heat and simmer for 5 minutes.
3. Stir in the olives, then lay the tilapia fillets in the sauce. Cook for about 8 minutes until the fish is cooked through.
4. Scatter with parsley and serve.

Per Serving

Calories: **282** | Fat: **15g** | Carbs: **6g** | Protein: **23g**

QUICK PRAWN JAMBALAYA

Prep time: **5 minutes** | Cook time: **25 minutes** | Serves **4**

- 1 shallot, finely chopped
- 250g gammon or ham, diced
- 400g tin chopped tomatoes
- 325ml vegetable stock
- 340g raw prawns, peeled
- Salt and freshly ground black pepper

1. Heat a little oil in a large saucepan over medium heat. Cook the shallots until softened, about 4 minutes.
2. Add the gammon, tomatoes and stock. Bring to the boil, then reduce heat and simmer, covered, for 13 minutes.
3. Add the prawns and cook for 3-4 minutes until they turn pink and the sauce has thickened slightly.
4. Season to taste and serve hot.

Per Serving

Calories: **170** | Fat: **4.8g** | Carbs: **5.6g** | Protein: **25.9g**

COD WITH MUSTARD CREAM

Prep time: **10 minutes** | Cook time: **10 minutes** | Serves **4**

For the fish:
- 1 tbsp coconut oil
- 4 cod fillets

For the sauce:
- 1 tsp English mustard
- 1 tsp paprika
- ¼ tsp ground bay leaves
- 3 tbsp full-fat soft cheese
- 125g Greek yoghurt
- Salt and freshly ground black pepper
- 6 basil leaves, finely shredded
- 1 garlic clove, finely chopped
- Finely grated zest of 1 lemon
- 2 tbsp fresh parsley, finely chopped
- Sea salt and freshly ground black pepper

1. Heat the coconut oil in a large frying pan over medium heat. Season the cod fillets and cook for 2-3 minutes on each side until just cooked through.
2. Meanwhile, mix all the sauce ingredients together until well combined.
3. Top each fillet with a portion of the sauce and garnish with the shredded basil leaves.

Per Serving

Calories: **166** | Fat: **8.2g** | Carbs: **2.6g** | Fiber: **0.3g** | Protein: **19.8g**

FISH AND SEAFOOD

STEAMED MUSSELS IN COCONUT CURRY

Prep time: **25 minutes** | Cook time: **10 minutes** | Serves **6**

- 1.5kg fresh mussels, cleaned and debearded
- 250g shallots, finely chopped
- 4 garlic cloves, finely chopped
- 400ml coconut milk
- 500ml dry white wine
- 2 tsp red curry powder
- 85ml coconut oil
- 4 spring onions, finely chopped
- Large handful fresh parsley, chopped

1. Pour the wine into a large saucepan and gently cook the shallots and garlic over low heat until softened.
2. Stir in the coconut milk and curry powder. Simmer for 3 minutes to combine the flavours.
3. Add the mussels, cover with a tight-fitting lid and steam for 7 minutes or until all the shells have opened. Using a slotted spoon, transfer the mussels to a serving bowl, discarding any that remain closed.
4. Stir the coconut oil into the cooking liquor, then remove from heat. Add the parsley and spring onions.
5. Pour the sauce over the mussels and serve immediately with butternut squash mash, if desired.

Per Serving

Calories: **356** | Fat: **20.6g** | Carbs: **0.3g** | Protein: **21.1g**

PAN-FRIED SALMON WITH TARRAGON MUSTARD SAUCE

Prep time: **15 minutes** | Cook time: **6 minutes** | Serves **4**

For the salmon:
- 4 salmon fillets
- ¾ tsp fresh thyme leaves
- 15g butter
- ¾ tsp fresh tarragon, chopped
- Salt and freshly ground black pepper

For the sauce:
- 65g Dijon mustard
- 30ml white wine
- 1 tsp fresh tarragon, chopped
- 65ml double cream

1. Season the salmon fillets with thyme, tarragon, salt and pepper.
2. Melt the butter in a large frying pan over medium heat. Add the salmon and cook for 4-5 minutes on each side until just cooked through. Transfer to warm plates and cover loosely with foil.
3. To make the sauce, add all sauce ingredients to the same pan over low heat. Simmer gently, stirring constantly, until slightly thickened.
4. Taste and adjust seasoning, then spoon over the salmon to serve.

Per Serving

Calories: **537** | Fat: **26.4g** | Carbs: **1.5g** | Protein: **67g**

ORIENTAL-STYLE FISH STEW

Prep time: **5 minutes** | Cook time: **20 minutes** | Serves **4**

- 1 tsp sesame oil
- 125g spring onions, thinly sliced
- 2cm piece fresh ginger, grated
- 2 garlic cloves, crushed
- 1 tsp red curry paste
- 2 whole star anise
- 1 tsp smoked paprika
- 2 ripe tomatoes, roughly chopped
- Sea salt and freshly ground black pepper
- 450g red snapper fillets, cut into chunks

1. Heat the sesame oil in a large saucepan over medium heat. Cook the spring onions until tender, then add ginger and garlic and cook for another minute, stirring frequently.
2. Add all remaining ingredients and reduce heat to medium-low.
3. Simmer gently for 15 minutes or until the fish flakes easily with a fork.

Per Serving

Calories: **151** | Fat: **3g** | Carbs: **5.8g** | Protein: **24.4g**

CHAPTER 8: VEGAN AND VEGETARIAN

VEGAN AND VEGETARIAN

CREAMED VEGETABLES

Prep time: **15 minutes** | Cook time: **6 hours** | Serves **6**

- 15ml extra-virgin olive oil
- ½ head cauliflower, cut into small florets
- 500g green beans, trimmed and cut into 5cm pieces
- 250g asparagus spears, trimmed and cut into 5cm pieces
- 125g crème fraîche
- 125g mature Cheddar cheese, grated
- 125g Gruyère cheese, grated
- 45g unsalted butter
- 65ml water
- ¼ tsp ground nutmeg
- Freshly ground black pepper, to taste

1. Lightly grease the slow cooker bowl with the olive oil.
2. Add the cauliflower, green beans, asparagus, crème fraîche, Cheddar, Gruyère, butter, water, nutmeg and pepper.
3. Cover and cook on low for 6 hours.
4. Season to taste and serve hot.

Per Serving:

Calories: **207** | Fat: **18g** | Protein: **8g** | Carbs: **5g**

SUNDAY CAULIFLOWER AND HAM GRATIN

Prep time: **5 minutes** | Cook time: **10 minutes** | Serves **6**

- 700g cauliflower, broken into small florets
- 125g Greek-style yoghurt
- 4 medium eggs, beaten
- 175g ham, diced
- 250g Gruyère cheese, freshly grated

1. Place the cauliflower in a large saucepan, cover with water and bring to the boil. Reduce the heat to medium-low immediately.
2. Simmer, covered, for approximately 6 minutes until tender. Drain thoroughly and mash with a potato masher.
3. Stir in the yoghurt, beaten eggs and ham until well combined.
4. Spoon the mixture into a lightly greased ovenproof dish. Top with the grated Gruyère.
5. Bake in a preheated oven at 180°C/160°C fan/gas mark 4 for 15-20 minutes until the cheese is golden and bubbling.

Per Serving

Calories: **236** | Fat: **13.8g** | Carbs: **7.2g** | Protein: **20.3g**

CREAMY BROCCOLI AND CAULIFLOWER BAKE

Prep time: **15 minutes** | Cook time: **6 hours** | Serves **6**

- 15ml extra-virgin olive oil
- 450g broccoli, cut into florets
- 450g cauliflower, cut into florets
- 65g ground almonds
- 500ml coconut milk
- ¼ tsp ground nutmeg
- Freshly ground black pepper, to taste
- 375g Gouda cheese, grated, divided

1. Lightly grease the slow cooker bowl with olive oil.
2. Place the broccoli and cauliflower in the bowl.
3. In a separate bowl, combine the ground almonds, coconut milk, nutmeg, pepper and 250g of the Gouda.
4. Pour the coconut milk mixture over the vegetables and top with the remaining 125g cheese.
5. Cover and cook on low for 6 hours.
6. Serve hot.

Per Serving:

Calories: **377** | Fat: **32g** | Protein: **16g** | Carbs: **12g**

CHAPTER 8

STUFFED SPAGHETTI SQUASH

Prep time: **5 minutes** | Cook time: **1 hour** | Serves **4**

- 225g spaghetti squash, halved and deseeded
- 10ml olive oil
- 125g mozzarella, grated
- 125g cream cheese
- 125g full-fat Greek yoghurt
- 2 medium eggs
- 1 garlic clove, finely chopped
- ⅛ tsp ground cumin
- ⅛ tsp dried basil
- ⅛ tsp dried mint
- Sea salt and freshly ground black pepper, to taste

1. Place the squash halves in a roasting tin and drizzle the cut sides with olive oil.
2. Bake in a preheated oven at 180°C/160°C fan/gas mark 4 for 45-50 minutes until tender when pierced with a fork.
3. Using a fork, scrape the squash flesh into "strands" and place in a mixing bowl. Add the remaining ingredients and mix well.
4. Spoon the mixture back into the squash shells and bake at 170°C/150°C fan/gas mark 3 for 5-10 minutes until the cheese is golden and bubbling.

Per Serving

Calories: **219** | Fat: **17.5g** | Carbs: **6.9g** | Fiber: **0.9g**

VEGETABLE AND TEMPEH KEBABS

Prep time: **2 hours 30 minutes** | Cook time: **15 minutes** | Serves **4**

- 280g tempeh, cut into chunks
- 375ml water
- 1 red onion, cut into chunks
- 1 red pepper, cut into chunks
- 1 yellow pepper, cut into chunks
- 2 tbsp olive oil
- 250g sugar-free barbecue sauce

1. Bring the water to the boil in a saucepan. Remove from heat, add the tempeh, cover and steam for 5 minutes to remove any bitterness.
2. Drain the tempeh and place in a bowl with the barbecue sauce, coating well. Cover and marinate in the fridge for 2 hours.
3. Preheat the barbecue or grill to medium-high heat (approximately 170°C).
4. Thread the tempeh, peppers and onion onto metal skewers.
5. Brush the barbecue grate with olive oil. Cook the kebabs for 3 minutes on each side, rotating and basting with additional barbecue sauce.
6. Serve hot with cauliflower couscous and tomato sauce.

Per Serving

Calories:**228** | Fat: **15g** | Carbs: **3.6g** | Protein: **13.2g**

CHEESY COURGETTE BITES

Prep time: **5 minutes** | Cook time: **40 minutes** | Serves **4**

- 5g sea salt
- 225g courgette, grated
- 125g ground almonds
- 2 medium eggs, beaten
- 250g Pecorino Romano cheese, grated

1. Place the grated courgette in a bowl with the salt. Leave for 15 minutes, then squeeze out excess liquid using a clean tea towel.
2. Mix in the ground almonds, eggs and Pecorino Romano. Grease a 12-hole mini-muffin tin with cooking spray.
3. Bake in a preheated oven at 180°C/160°C fan/gas mark 4 for 15 minutes until set. Allow to cool for 5 minutes before serving.

Per Serving

Calories: **224** | Fat: **18g** | Carbs: **3g** | Protein: **13.4g**

VEGAN AND VEGETARIAN

CAULIFLOWER, CHEESE AND SPRING GREENS WAFFLES

Prep time: 45 minutes | **Cook time: 5 minutes** | Serves **4**

- 2 spring onions, finely chopped
- 15ml olive oil
- 2 medium eggs
- 80g Parmesan, freshly grated
- 250g spring greens, chopped
- 250g mozzarella, grated
- ½ cauliflower head
- 5g garlic powder
- 15g sesame seeds
- 10g fresh thyme, chopped

1. Place the cauliflower in a food processor and blitz until it resembles rice. Add the spring greens, spring onions and thyme. Pulse until smooth. Transfer to a bowl.
2. Stir in the remaining ingredients until well combined.
3. Heat a waffle iron and spread the mixture evenly. Cook according to the manufacturer's instructions.

Per Serving

Calories: **283** | Carbs: **3.5g** | Fat: **20.3g** | Protein: **16g**

BROCCOLI, MINT AND CHEDDAR SOUP

Prep time: 20 minutes | **Cook time: 11 minutes** | Serves **4**

- 185g double cream
- 1 onion, finely chopped
- 2 cloves garlic, finely chopped
- 1kg broccoli, chopped
- 1L vegetable stock
- 30g butter
- 800g mature Cheddar, grated, plus 65g for garnish
- Salt and freshly ground black pepper
- ½ bunch fresh mint, chopped

1. Melt the butter in a large saucepan over medium heat.
2. Sauté the onion and garlic for 3 minutes until softened, stirring occasionally. Season with salt and pepper. Add the stock and broccoli, bring to the boil. Reduce the heat and simmer for 10 minutes.
3. Blend the soup until smooth using a stick blender. Stir in the cheese and cook until creamy, about 1 minute. Check seasoning. Stir in the double cream. Serve in bowls topped with the reserved Cheddar and fresh mint.

Per Serving

Calories: **561** | Carbs: **7g** | Fat: **52.3g** | Protein: **24g**

COURGETTI WITH AVOCADO AND PESTO

Prep time: 15 minutes | **Cook time: 4 minutes** | Serves **4**

- 4 large courgettes, spiralised
- 125g fresh pesto
- 2 ripe avocados, sliced
- 250g Kalamata olives, roughly chopped
- 65g fresh basil, chopped
- 30ml olive oil
- 65g sun-dried tomatoes, chopped

1. Heat half the olive oil in a large frying pan over medium heat. Add the courgetti and cook for 4 minutes.
2. Transfer to a serving plate. Stir in the remaining olive oil, pesto, basil, sun-dried tomatoes and olives.
3. Top with avocado slices and serve.

Per Serving

Calories: **449** | Carbs: **8.4g** | Fat: **42g** | Protein: **6.3g**

CHAPTER 8

CAULIFLOWER AND AVOCADO WRAPS

Prep time: **5 minutes** | Cook time: **5 minutes** | Serves **4**

- 30g butter
- ½ head cauliflower, broken into florets
- 4 low-carb tortilla wraps
- 250g natural yoghurt
- 250g fresh tomato salsa
- 1 ripe avocado, sliced
- 15g fresh basil, chopped

1. Place the cauliflower in a food processor and pulse until it resembles rice. Melt the butter in a frying pan and add the cauliflower rice. Sauté for 4-5 minutes until tender. Season with salt and pepper.
2. Spread each wrap with yoghurt and top with salsa. Add the cauliflower rice, avocado slices and basil. Roll up the wraps and cut each in half diagonally.

Per Serving

Calories: **457** | Fat: **31.3g** | Carbs: **9.6g** | Protein: **15.8g**

COURGETTI WITH AVOCADO AND OLIVES

Prep time: **15 minutes** | Cook time: **5 minutes** | Serves **4**

- 4 courgettes, spiralised
- 125g fresh pesto
- 2 ripe avocados, sliced
- 200g Kalamata olives, roughly chopped
- 65g fresh basil, chopped
- 15ml olive oil
- 65g sun-dried tomatoes, chopped
- Salt and freshly ground black pepper

1. Heat half the olive oil in a large frying pan over medium heat. Add the courgetti and cook for 4 minutes.
2. Transfer to a serving plate. Stir in the pesto, basil, sun-dried tomatoes and olives. Season to taste.
3. Top with avocado slices to serve.

Per Serving

Calories: **449** | Fat: **42g** | Carbs: **8.4g** | Protein: **6.3g**

MUSHROOM RISOTTO WITH CAULIFLOWER RICE

Prep time: **15 minutes** | Cook time: **7 minutes** | Serves **4**

- 2 shallots, finely chopped
- 45ml olive oil
- 65ml vegetable stock
- 80g Parmesan, freshly grated
- 60g butter
- 40g fresh chives, finely chopped
- 900g mushrooms, sliced
- 1.25kg cauliflower, riced

1. Heat 30ml oil in a large saucepan. Add the mushrooms and cook over medium heat for about 3 minutes. Remove from the pan and set aside.
2. Heat the remaining oil and cook the shallots for 2 minutes. Add the cauliflower rice and stock, and cook until the liquid is absorbed. Stir in the remaining ingredients.

Per Serving

Calories: **264** | Carbs: **8.4g** | Fat: **18g** | Protein: **11g**

VEGAN AND VEGETARIAN

ROASTED CAULIFLOWER GRATIN

Prep time: **21 minutes** | Cook time: **18 minutes** | Serves **4**

- 80g butter, plus 30g melted
- 1 onion, finely chopped
- 2 heads cauliflower, cut into florets
- Salt and freshly ground black pepper
- 65ml almond milk
- 125g ground almonds
- 375g mature Cheddar, grated
- 15g flaked almonds
- 15g fresh parsley, chopped

1. Steam the cauliflower in salted water for 4-5 minutes. Drain well and set aside.
2. Melt the 80g butter in a large saucepan over medium heat and sauté the onion for 3 minutes.
3. Add the cauliflower, season with salt and pepper, and stir in the almond milk.
4. Simmer for 3 minutes.
5. Mix the remaining melted butter with the ground almonds. Stir into the cauliflower along with half the cheese. Transfer to an ovenproof dish, top with remaining cheese and flaked almonds.
6. Bake in a preheated oven at 180°C/160°C fan/gas mark 4 for 10 minutes until golden brown. Garnish with parsley to serve.

Per Serving

Calories: **455** | Fat: **38.3g** | Carbs: **6.5g** | Protein: **16.3g**

SPANISH-STYLE STUFFED PEPPERS

Prep time: **5 minutes** | Cook time: **25 minutes** | Serves **4**

- 15ml olive oil
- 1 Spanish onion, finely chopped
- 2 cloves garlic, crushed
- 250ml vegetable stock
- 225g chorizo sausage, finely diced
- 1 large ripe tomato, chopped
- 225g ricotta
- Sea salt and freshly ground black pepper
- 4 red peppers, halved and deseeded
- 55g Gruyère, grated

1. Heat the olive oil in a frying pan over medium heat. Sauté the onion and garlic for 2 minutes until softened and fragrant.
2. Add a splash of stock to deglaze the pan. Stir in the chorizo, tomato and ricotta. Season to taste.
3. Place the pepper halves in a microwaveable dish and cook for 8 minutes until slightly softened.
4. Fill the pepper halves with the chorizo mixture and place in a lightly oiled ovenproof dish. Pour the remaining stock around the peppers.
5. Bake in a preheated oven at 210°C/190°C fan/gas mark 7 for 9 minutes. Top with Gruyère and bake for a further 4-5 minutes until the cheese is golden and bubbling.

Per Serving

Calories: **340** | Fat: **27.2g** | Carbs: **5.2g** | Protein: **14.7g**

AVOCADO AND TOMATO WRAPS

Prep time: **5 minutes** | Cook time: **2 minutes** | Serves **4**

- 500g cauliflower rice
- 6 low-carb tortilla wraps
- 500g soured cream
- 375g tomato and herb salsa
- 2 ripe avocados, peeled, stoned and sliced

1. Place the cauliflower rice in a microwave-safe bowl, sprinkle with a little water, and microwave for 2 minutes until tender. Spread each wrap with soured cream and top with salsa.
2. Divide the cauliflower rice between the wraps and layer the avocado slices on top. Fold in the sides and roll up tightly, then cut each wrap in half diagonally.

Per Serving

Calories: **303** | Fat: **25g** | Carbs: **6g** | Protein: **8g**

CHAPTER 8

COURGETTE AND SPINACH LASAGNE

Prep time: **40 minutes** | Cook time: **35 minutes** | Serves **4**

- 2 large courgettes, thinly sliced lengthways
- Salt and freshly ground black pepper
- 500g feta cheese
- 500g mozzarella, grated
- 750g passata
- 250g baby spinach
- 1 tbsp fresh basil, chopped

1. Mix the feta, mozzarella, salt and pepper. Spread 65g of the cheese mixture in the base of a greased ovenproof dish. Layer one-third of the courgette slices, followed by 250g passata and 80g spinach.
2. Repeat the layering twice more, finishing with the remaining 65g cheese mixture.
3. Bake in a preheated oven at 180°C/160°C fan/gas mark 4 for 35 minutes until golden brown. Rest for 5 minutes before serving garnished with basil.

Per Serving

Calories: **411** | Fat: **41.3g** | Carbs: **3.2g** | Protein: **6.5g**

SPICY WARM CABBAGE SALAD

Prep time: **5 minutes** | Cook time: **45 minutes** | Serves **4**

- 3 tbsp extra virgin olive oil
- 1 medium leek, finely sliced
- 225g green cabbage, shredded
- 1g caraway seeds
- Sea salt, to taste
- 4-5 black peppercorns, crushed
- 1 garlic clove, finely chopped
- 5g English mustard
- 14g balsamic vinegar
- A few drops of hot chilli sauce

1. Preheat the oven to 210°C/190°C fan/Gas mark 6-7. Drizzle 2 tablespoons of olive oil over the leek and cabbage; sprinkle with caraway seeds, salt and crushed peppercorns.
2. Roast for 37-40 minutes until the edges are crispy and golden. Transfer the roasted vegetables to a serving bowl.
3. Toss with the remaining olive oil, garlic, mustard, vinegar and chilli sauce. Serve whilst hot.

Per Serving

Calories: **118** | Fat: **10.2g** | Carbs: **6.6g** | Protein: **1.1g**

CREAMY BRAISED KALE

Prep time: **5 minutes** | Cook time: **15 minutes** | Serves **5**

- 1 tbsp olive oil
- 1 banana shallot, finely chopped
- 2.7kg kale, stems removed and leaves torn
- 1g fresh garlic, finely chopped
- 2 tbsp dry white wine
- 1g dried chilli flakes
- Sea salt and freshly ground black pepper, to taste
- 125ml double cream

1. Heat the olive oil in a large, heavy-based pan over medium heat. Gently fry the shallot until softened, about 4 minutes.
2. Add the kale and cook for 2 minutes more. Drain any excess liquid and stir in the garlic; cook for another minute.
3. Pour in the wine to deglaze the pan. Add the chilli flakes, season with salt and pepper, then stir in the double cream.
4. Reduce heat to low, cover and simmer for 4 minutes until the kale is tender. Serve hot.

Per Serving

Calories: **130** | Fat: **10.5g** | Carbs: **6.1g** | Protein: **3.7g**

VEGAN AND VEGETARIAN

INDIAN-SPICED CABBAGE STIR-FRY

Prep time: **5 minutes** | Cook time: **25 minutes** | Serves **4**

- 2 tbsp olive oil
- 2.5cm piece fresh root ginger, grated
- 1g cumin seeds
- 1 banana shallot, finely chopped
- 125ml chicken stock
- 340g green cabbage, finely sliced
- 1g ground turmeric
- 1g ground coriander
- Salt and cayenne pepper, to taste

1. Heat the olive oil in a large frying pan over medium heat; fry the ginger and cumin seeds until fragrant.
2. Add the shallot and cook for 2-3 minutes until softened and aromatic. Pour in the chicken stock to deglaze the pan.
3. Stir in the cabbage, turmeric, ground coriander, salt and cayenne pepper. Cover and cook for 15-18 minutes until the cabbage is tender, stirring occasionally.
4. Divide between serving bowls and serve immediately.

Per Serving

Calories: **168** | Fat: **13g** | Carbs: **7g** | Protein: **2.6g**

CAULIFLOWER GOUDA CASSEROLE

Prep time: **21 minutes** | Cook time: **11 minutes** | Serves **4**

- 2 cauliflower heads, cut into florets
- 85g butter, plus 28g melted
- 1 white onion, finely chopped
- Salt and freshly ground black pepper, to taste
- 60ml almond milk
- 125g ground almonds
- 375g Gouda cheese, grated

1. Preheat the oven to 170°C/150°C fan/Gas mark 3. Place the cauliflower florets in a large microwave-safe bowl, sprinkle with a little water, and microwave for 4-5 minutes until just tender.
2. Melt the 85g butter in a large saucepan over medium heat and cook the onion for 3 minutes until softened. Add the cauliflower, season with salt and pepper, then pour in the almond milk. Simmer for 3 minutes.
3. Mix the remaining melted butter with the ground almonds. Stir this mixture into the cauliflower along with half the cheese. Transfer to an ovenproof dish, sprinkle with the remaining cheese and bake for 10 minutes until golden and bubbling. Serve hot with a crisp green salad.

Per Serving

Calories:**215** | Fat: **15g** | Carbs: **4g** | Protein: **12g**

BROCCOLI AND CHEESE CROQUETTES

Prep time: **5 minutes** | Cook time: **15 minutes** | Serves **5**

- 450g broccoli florets
- 14g fresh parsley, finely chopped
- 1g paprika
- Sea salt and freshly ground black pepper
- 3 large eggs
- 250g Pecorino Romano cheese, freshly grated
- 140g Swiss cheese, sliced
- 2 tbsp olive oil

1. Pulse the broccoli in a food processor until it resembles rice-sized pieces.
2. Mix the broccoli with parsley, paprika, seasoning, eggs and Pecorino Romano. Shape into patties.
3. Heat the olive oil in a large frying pan over medium heat.
4. Cook the croquettes for 4-5 minutes, top with Swiss cheese, then carefully flip and cook for a further 4 minutes until golden and cooked through.

Per Serving

Calories: **323** | Fat: **24.1g** | Carbs: **5.9g** | Protein: **19.8g**

CHAPTER 8

CHESTNUT MUSHROOM STROGANOFF

Prep time: **25 minutes** | Cook time: **15 minutes** | Serves **4**

- 40g butter
- 1 white onion, finely chopped
- 1kg chestnut mushrooms, thickly sliced
- 500ml water
- 125ml double cream
- 125g Parmesan cheese, freshly grated
- 20g mixed dried herbs
- Salt and freshly ground black pepper

1. Melt the butter in a large frying pan over medium heat. Add the onion and cook for 3 minutes until softened.
2. Add the mushrooms and cook for 5 minutes until tender. Pour in the water, bring to the boil and simmer for 10-15 minutes until slightly reduced.
3. Stir in the double cream and Parmesan cheese until the cheese melts. Add the dried herbs and season well with salt and pepper. Simmer for 5 minutes.
4. Serve hot over spiralised courgettes.

Per Serving

Calories:**284** | Fat: **28g** | Carbs: **1,5g** | Protein: **8g**

CREAMY VEGETABLE STEW

Prep time: **32 minutes** | Cook time: **25 minutes** | Serves **4**

- 28g ghee
- 14g onion and garlic paste
- 4 medium carrots, roughly chopped
- 1 large cauliflower, broken into florets
- 500g green beans, topped and tailed
- Salt and freshly ground black pepper
- 250ml water
- 375ml double cream

1. Melt the ghee in a large saucepan over medium heat and fry the onion and garlic paste until fragrant, about 2 minutes.
2. Add the carrots, cauliflower, and green beans. Season with salt and pepper, pour in the water, and stir well. Reduce the heat to low, cover and simmer for 25 minutes until the vegetables are tender.
3. Stir in the double cream and warm through. Adjust the seasoning to taste. Serve hot with low-carb bread.

Per Serving

Calories:**310** | Fat: **26.4g** | Carbs: **6g** | Protein: **8g**

SWISS CHEESE AND BROCCOLI BAKE

Prep time: **5 minutes** | Cook time: **25 minutes** | Serves **5**

- 3 tbsp olive oil
- 5g garlic, finely chopped
- 750g broccoli florets
- 1g sea salt flakes
- 1g freshly ground black pepper
- 1g paprika
- 125g condensed mushroom soup
- 170g Swiss cheese, grated

1. Heat 1 tbsp olive oil in a non-stick frying pan over medium heat. Gently fry the garlic until softened and fragrant.
2. Preheat the oven to 180°C/160°C fan/Gas mark 4. Brush an ovenproof dish with 1 tbsp olive oil.
3. Cook the broccoli in boiling salted water until just tender. Drain well and transfer to the prepared dish. Scatter over the sautéed garlic.
4. Drizzle with the remaining oil and season with salt, pepper and paprika. Pour over the mushroom soup.
5. Top with the grated Swiss cheese and bake for about 18 minutes until bubbling and golden.

Per Serving

Calories: **179** | Fat: **10.3g** | Carbs: **7.6g** | Protein: **13.5g**

CHAPTER 9:
DESSERTS

CHAPTER 9

FIVE-SEED CRACKERS

Prep time: **5 minutes** | Cook time: **2 hours** | Serves **12**

- 65g chia seeds
- 65g sesame seeds
- 65g linseeds
- 65g sunflower seeds
- 65g pumpkin seeds
- 65g ground almonds
- 5g psyllium husk powder
- Coarse sea salt, to taste
- 1 teaspoon ground cumin
- 185ml boiling water
- 4 tablespoons coconut oil, melted

1. Preheat the oven to 155°C (fan 135°C/gas mark 2).
2. In a large bowl, combine all seeds, ground almonds, psyllium husk powder, salt, and cumin.
3. Pour over the boiling water and melted coconut oil, stirring well to combine.
4. Spread the mixture thinly on a baking tray lined with foil.
5. Bake for 30 minutes, then rotate the tray and bake for a further 25-30 minutes.
6. Turn off the oven and leave the crackers inside to dry for 50-60 minutes.

Per Serving

Calories: **128** | Fat: **12.3g** | Carbs: **3.1g** | Protein: **3.3g**

CHEDDAR AND CHIVE SCONES

Prep time: **15 minutes** | Cook time: **15 minutes** | Serves **8**

- 250g plain flour
- 1 tablespoon baking powder
- ½ teaspoon salt
- 50g unsalted butter, chilled and cubed
- 100g mature cheddar cheese, grated
- 3 tablespoons fresh chives, chopped
- 150ml milk
- 1 large egg (for glazing)

1. Preheat your oven to 220°C (200°C fan) and line a baking tray with baking paper.
2. In a large bowl, sift the plain flour, baking powder, and salt together. Add the cubed butter and rub it into the flour until the mixture resembles breadcrumbs. Stir in the grated cheddar and chopped chives.
3. Make a well in the centre of the mixture and pour in the milk. Mix gently until a soft dough forms. Be careful not to overwork the dough.
4. Turn the dough out onto a lightly floured surface. Gently roll out to about 2cm thick. Use a round cutter (about 5cm in diameter) to cut out scones and place them on the prepared baking tray.
5. Beat the egg and brush it over the tops of the scones for a shiny finish. Bake in the preheated oven for 12-15 minutes, or until golden brown and well risen.
6. Allow to cool slightly before serving. These scones are best enjoyed warm, but they can also be stored in an airtight container for a couple of days.

Per Serving

Calories: **180** | Fat: **9g** | Carbs: **19g** | Protein: **5g**

LAYERED BERRY AND AVOCADO FOOL

Prep time: **3 minutes** | Cook time: **1 minutes** | Serves **4**

- 125g walnuts, toasted
- 1 ripe avocado, peeled and diced
- 250g cream cheese, softened
- 250g fresh blueberries
- 250g fresh raspberries
- 250g fresh blackberries

1. Layer half the cream cheese, mixed berries, walnuts and avocado in dessert glasses.
2. Repeat the layers with remaining ingredients.
3. Cover with cling film and refrigerate for 1 hour until firm.

Per Serving

Calories:**322** | Fat: **28.3g** | Carbs:**6.5g** | Protein: **9g**

DESSERTS

FROZEN BLUEBERRY PEARLS

Prep time: 12 minutes | Cook time: 5 minutes | Serves 4

- 3g vanilla extract
- 2 sheets leaf gelatine
- 30ml double cream
- 500ml water
- 40g blueberries, crushed
- 500g crushed ice
- 250ml cold water

1. Heat the water in a saucepan until just boiling. Take off the heat and add the pre-soaked gelatine, stirring until completely dissolved.
2. Pour into a blender with the remaining ingredients and blitz until smooth.
3. Pour into small round ice moulds and freeze for at least 3 hours until solid.

Per Serving

Calories: **142** | Fat: **9g** | Carbs: **7.8g** | Protein: **3.5g**

EASY EVERYDAY BROWNIES

Prep time: 5 minutes | Cook time: 25 minutes | Serves 10

- 125ml unsalted butter, melted
- 350g coconut flour
- 5g baking powder
- 80g unsweetened cocoa powder
- 250g xylitol

1. Preheat the oven to 180°C (160°C fan). In a large bowl, mix all the ingredients in the order listed.
2. Pour the batter into a parchment-lined baking tin.
3. Bake for approximately 20 minutes, or until a skewer inserted into the centre comes out clean.
4. Cool on a wire rack for 1 hour before slicing and serving. Enjoy!

Per Serving

Calories: **123** | Fat: **12.9g** | Carbs: **3.1g** | Protein: **0.9g**

SLOW-COOKER BLUEBERRY CRUMBLE

Prep time: 10 minutes | Cook time: 3 to 4 hours | Serves 8

For the filling:
- 1kg blueberries
- 2 tbsp granulated sweetener (erythritol)

For the crumble:
- 185g granulated sweetener (erythritol)
- 250g ground pecans
- 5g bicarbonate of soda
- 3g ground cinnamon
- 15g coconut oil, melted
- 30ml coconut milk
- 1 large egg
- 45g coconut oil, melted

1. Lightly grease a slow cooker bowl with some of the melted coconut oil.
2. Toss the blueberries with 2 tablespoons of sweetener and place in the slow cooker.
3. In a large bowl, mix together the remaining sweetener, ground pecans, bicarbonate of soda and cinnamon.
4. Stir in the coconut milk, egg and remaining melted coconut oil until the mixture resembles coarse breadcrumbs.
5. Spread the crumble mixture evenly over the blueberries.
6. Cover and cook on low for 3-4 hours.
7. Serve warm.

Per Serving

Calories: **222** | Fat: **19g** | Protein: **9g** | Carbs: **9g**

CHAPTER 9

KETO BREAD

Prep time: **5 minutes** | Cook time: **40 minutes** | Serves **10**

- 1g cream of tartar
- 6 large egg whites
- 375g almond flour
- 4 tablespoons melted butter
- 4g baking soda
- 15ml apple cider vinegar
- 2 tablespoons coconut flour

1. Preheat the oven to 187°C (fan 167°C). Grease an 8 x 4-inch loaf tin.
2. In a medium bowl, combine the cream of tartar and egg whites. Beat with an electric mixer until soft peaks form.
3. In a food processor, blend together the almond flour, melted butter, baking soda, apple cider vinegar, and coconut flour.
4. Transfer the mixture to a large bowl and gently fold in the egg whites.
5. Pour the batter into the loaf tin and bake for 30 minutes.
6. Remove from the oven and allow to cool for 10 minutes before serving. Store in the refrigerator.

Per Serving

Calories: **44** | Fat: **3.5g** | Protein: **1.8g** | Carbs: **1.6g**

MINI MUFFINS ON THE GO

Prep time: **5 minutes** | Cook time: **40 minutes** | Serves **6**

- 2 rashers streaky bacon, cooked and finely chopped
- 125g spring onions, finely chopped
- 1 garlic clove, crushed
- 250g kale, finely shredded
- 4 large free-range eggs, well beaten
- 4 tablespoons Greek yoghurt
- Sea salt and white pepper, to taste

1. Preheat the oven to 180°C (fan 160°C/gas mark 4). Line a mini muffin tin with paper cases.
2. In a large bowl, combine the bacon, spring onions, garlic, and kale.
3. Fold in the beaten eggs and yoghurt until well combined.
4. Season with salt and white pepper, then divide the mixture between the paper cases.
5. Bake for 30 minutes or until firm to the touch.
6. Leave to cool for 5 minutes, then carefully run a palette knife around each muffin to release. Serve warm or at room temperature.

Per Serving

Calories: **88** | Fat: **6.5g** | Carbs: **1.7g** | Protein: **5.4g**

CHEESY CAULIFLOWER FRITTERS

Prep time: **35 minutes** | Cook time: **13 minutes** | Serves **4**

- 450g grated cauliflower
- 125g grated Parmesan cheese
- 85g chopped onion
- 3g baking powder
- 125g almond flour
- 2 medium eggs
- 3ml lemon juice
- 28ml olive oil
- 5g sea salt

1. Sprinkle salt over the cauliflower in a bowl and let it sit for 10 minutes. Add the remaining ingredients, then mix with your hands until well combined.
2. Heat a skillet over medium heat with the olive oil. Shape the mixture into small fritters.
3. Fry in batches, cooking each side for about 3 minutes or until golden brown.

Per Serving

Calories:**69** | Fat: **4.5g** | Carbs: **3g** | Protein: **4.5g**

DESSERTS

SLOW-COOKER LEMON POSSET

Prep time: **10 minutes** | Cook time: **3 hours** | Serves **4**

- 5 egg yolks
- 65ml fresh lemon juice
- 14g lemon zest
- 5g vanilla extract
- 2ml liquid stevia
- 500ml double cream
- 250ml whipped coconut cream, to serve

1. Whisk together the egg yolks, lemon juice and zest, vanilla and liquid stevia in a medium bowl.
2. Stir in the double cream and divide between 4 (125ml) ramekins.
3. Place a trivet in the base of the slow cooker and arrange the ramekins on top.
4. Pour in enough hot water to come halfway up the sides of the ramekins.
5. Cover and cook on low for 3 hours.
6. Remove the ramekins carefully and cool to room temperature.
7. Chill thoroughly in the fridge and serve topped with whipped coconut cream.

Per Serving

Calories: **319** | Fat: **30g** | Protein: **7g** | Carbs: **3g**

MATCHA AND MACADAMIA SQUARES

Prep time: **28 minutes** | Cook time: **18 minutes** | Serves **4**

- 14g matcha green tea powder
- 65g unsalted butter, melted
- 56g sugar-free icing sugar alternative
- Pinch of salt
- 65g coconut flour
- 3g baking powder
- 1 large egg
- 125g pistachios, roughly chopped

1. Preheat the oven to 175°C/155°C fan/Gas mark 4. Line a 20cm square tin with baking parchment.
2. In a bowl, whisk together the melted butter, sugar alternative and salt. Beat in the egg until well combined.
3. Sift together the coconut flour, matcha powder and baking powder, then fold into the wet ingredients.
4. Stir in the pistachios and pour into the prepared tin.
5. Bake for 18 minutes until just set. Cool completely before cutting into squares.

Per Serving

Calories: **243** | Fat: **22g** | Carbs: **4.3g** | Protein: **7.2g**

CITRUS MOUSSE WITH TOASTED ALMONDS

Prep time: **5 minutes** | Cook time: **5 minutes** | Serves **4**

- 340g cream cheese, softened
- 500g sugar-free icing sugar alternative
- 1 lemon, juice and zest
- 1 lime, juice and zest
- Pinch of salt
- 250ml whipping cream, plus extra for decoration
- 65g flaked almonds, toasted

1. Using an electric hand whisk, beat the cream cheese until light and fluffy. Beat in the sugar alternative, citrus juices and salt until well combined. Fold in the whipped cream.
2. Divide between serving glasses and chill for 1 hour until set.
3. Top with extra whipped cream, citrus zest and toasted almonds just before serving.

Per Serving

Calories: **242** | Fat: **18g** | Carbs: **3.3g** | Protein: **6.5g**

CHAPTER 9

BLUEBERRY TART WITH LAVENDER

Prep time: **35 minutes** | Cook time: **30 minutes** | Serves **6**

- 1 large low-carb pie crust
- 375ml double cream
- 28g Swerve
- 14g culinary lavender
- 1 tsp vanilla extract
- 500g fresh blueberries
- Erythritol for topping

1. Preheat the oven to 200°C (180°C fan). Place the pie crust on a baking tray and bake for 30 minutes or until golden brown. Remove and allow to cool.
2. In a saucepan, combine the double cream and lavender, bringing the mixture to a gentle boil. Remove from heat, let cool, then strain the lavender from the cream. Add Swerve and vanilla, stirring to combine, then pour the mixture into the cooled crust.
3. Scatter the blueberries on top and refrigerate for 45 minutes before serving. Finish with a sprinkle of erythritol.

Per Serving

Calories: **198** | Fat: **16.4g** | Carbs: **10.7g** | Protein: **3.3g**

VANILLA FLAN WITH MINT

Prep time: **60 minutes** | Cook time: **45 to 50 minutes** | Serves **4**

- 85g erythritol, for caramel
- 500ml almond milk
- 4 large eggs
- 1 tsp vanilla extract
- Zest of 1 lemon
- 125g erythritol, for custard
- 500ml double cream
- Fresh mint leaves, to serve

1. Heat the erythritol for the caramel in a deep pan, adding 2-3 tablespoons of water. Bring to a boil, then reduce heat and simmer until golden. Divide the caramel among 4-6 metal tins and set aside to cool.
2. In a bowl, whisk together the eggs, remaining erythritol, lemon zest, and vanilla. Add the almond milk and mix until well combined. Pour the custard into each caramel-lined ramekin and place in a deep baking tin.
3. Fill the tin halfway with hot water. Bake at 170°C (150°C fan) for 45-50 minutes. Allow the flans to cool, then refrigerate for at least 4 hours. Run a knife around the edges to release, and serve with whipped cream and a sprinkle of fresh mint.

Per Serving

Calories: **269** | Fat: **26g** | Carbs: **1.7g** | Protein: **7.6g**

LEMON CHEESECAKE MOUSSE

Prep time: **5 minutes + cooling time** | Serves **4**

- 680g cream cheese, softened
- 500g Swerve confectioner's sugar
- Juice and zest of 2 lemons
- Pink salt, to taste
- 250ml whipped cream, plus extra for garnish

1. In a large bowl, use a hand mixer to whip the cream cheese until light and fluffy. Mix in the Swerve, lemon juice, and salt, then fold in the whipped cream until smooth and combined.
2. Spoon the mousse into serving cups and refrigerate for 1 hour to thicken. Top with a swirl of extra whipped cream and a sprinkle of lemon zest just before serving.

Per Serving

Calories: **223** | Fat: **18g** | Carbs: **3g** | Protein: **12g**

DESSERTS

GREEN TEA BROWNIES WITH MACADAMIA NUTS

Prep time: 28 minutes | **Cook time:** 18 minutes | Serves 4

- 14g matcha (green tea) powder
- 65g unsalted butter, melted
- 56g Swerve confectioner's sugar
- A pinch of sea salt
- 65g coconut flour
- 3g baking powder
- 1 large egg
- 65g chopped macadamia nuts

1. Preheat the oven to 170°C (150°C fan). Line a square baking dish with parchment paper. In a bowl, whisk together the melted butter, Swerve, and salt, then beat in the egg until incorporated.
2. Sift the coconut flour, matcha powder, and baking powder into the wet mixture, stirring to combine. Fold in the chopped macadamia nuts.
3. Pour the mixture into the prepared baking dish and bake for 18 minutes. Allow to cool slightly, then cut into squares.

Per Serving

Calories: **248** | Fat: **23.1g** | Carbs: **2.2g** | Protein: **5.2g**

GRANDMA'S COCONUT TREATS

Prep time: 3 hours | **Cook time:** 40 minutes | Serves 4

- 80g ghee
- 10 saffron threads
- 350ml coconut milk, divided
- 450g shredded coconut
- 56g xylitol
- 5g ground cardamom

1. In a bowl, combine the shredded coconut with half of the coconut milk. In another bowl, mix the remaining coconut milk with the xylitol and saffron threads, then set aside for 30 minutes.
2. Heat the ghee in a wok over low heat. Add both coconut mixtures, stirring continuously for 5 minutes. Mix in the ground cardamom and cook for an additional 5 minutes.
3. Spread the mixture into a small container and freeze for 2 hours. Cut into bars to serve.

Per Serving

Calories: **224** | Fat: **21.7g** | Carbs: **2.7g** | Protein: **3.3g**

EGGLESS STRAWBERRY MOUSSE

Prep time: 6 minutes plus cooling | **Cook time:** 10 minutes | Serves 6

- 500ml double cream, chilled
- 500g fresh strawberries, hulled
- 70g erythritol
- 28ml lemon juice
- 1g strawberry extract
- 28g sugar-free strawberry preserves

1. In a large bowl, whip the double cream on high speed with a hand mixer until stiff peaks form, about 1 minute; refrigerate immediately. Puree the strawberries in a blender, then transfer to a saucepan.
2. Add erythritol and lemon juice, cooking over low heat for 3 minutes, stirring constantly. Stir in the strawberry extract, turn off the heat, and allow to cool. Gently fold in the whipped cream until well incorporated, then spoon into six ramekins. Chill for 4 hours until set.
3. Garnish with strawberry preserves just before serving.

Per Serving

Calories: **290** | Fat: **24g** | Carbs: **5g** | Protein: **5g**

CHAPTER 9

COCONUT BARS

Prep time: **10 minutes** | Cook time: **15 minutes** | Serves **4**

- 100g ghee
- 10 saffron threads
- 300ml coconut milk, divided
- 350g shredded coconut
- 56g sweetener of choice
- 5g ground cardamom

1. In a bowl, combine the shredded coconut with 250ml of coconut milk. In another bowl, mix the remaining coconut milk with the sweetener and saffron, and let it sit for 30 minutes.
2. Heat the ghee in a wok over low heat. Add the coconut mixtures, stirring for 5 minutes. Mix in the cardamom and cook for an additional 5 minutes.
3. Spread the mixture into a small container, then freeze for 2 hours. Slice into bars and serve.

Per Serving

Calories: **215** | Fat: **22g** | Carbs: **1.4g** | Protein: **2g**

VANILLA PUDDING WITH HAZELNUTS

Prep time: **5 minutes** | Cook time: **10 minutes** | Serves **4**

- 250ml double cream
- 1/10 tsp Swerve
- 4 tbsp cream cheese
- 1/10 tsp vanilla extract
- 115g ground hazelnuts

1. Place a mixing bowl in the freezer for 5-10 minutes to chill.
2. Remove the bowl from the freezer, pour in the double cream, and beat on high speed until it begins to thicken. Gradually add the Swerve, beating until stiff peaks form.
3. Fold in the cream cheese and vanilla extract, mixing until smooth. Carefully fold in the ground hazelnuts.
4. Serve well chilled and enjoy!

Per Serving

Calories: **341** | Fat: **33.2g** | Carbs: **7.6g** | Protein: **6.6g**

NO-BAKE RAW COCONUT BALLS

Prep time: **22 minutes** | Cook time: **20 minutes** | Serves **4**

- 1g coconut extract
- 160g melted coconut oil
- 400ml coconut milk
- 16 drops liquid stevia
- 250g unsweetened coconut flakes

1. In a large bowl, mix the melted coconut oil, coconut milk, coconut extract, and stevia. Add the coconut flakes, stirring until evenly coated.
2. Spoon the mixture into silicone muffin moulds and freeze for 1 hour to set.

Per Serving

Calories: **211** | Fat: **19g** | Carbs: **2.2g** | Protein: **2.9g**

DESSERTS

KETO FUDGE

Prep time: **5 minutes** | Cook time: **3 hours** | Serves **10**

- 250g full-fat coconut cream
- 65g powdered monk fruit sweetener
- 10g vanilla extract
- 2 tbsp butter, at room temperature
- 250g stevia-sweetened dark chocolate chips

1. Line a loaf tin with parchment paper.
2. In a small saucepan over medium heat, combine the coconut cream, monk fruit sweetener, and vanilla extract. Bring to a simmer, stirring often, for 20 minutes, or until reduced by nearly half and thickened to a condensed milk consistency.
3. Reduce the heat to low and stir in the butter until melted.
4. Add the dark chocolate chips and stir until fully melted.
5. Pour the mixture into the prepared loaf tin and refrigerate for at least 2 hours, or until set. Turn out onto a wooden cutting board and cut into 1-inch square pieces. Store in the refrigerator.

Per Serving

Calories: **166** | Fat: **14.4g** | Protein: **2.2g** | Carbs: **17.4g**

KETO PEANUT BUTTER COOKIES

Prep time: **5 minutes** | Cook time: **22 minutes** | Serves **12**

- 250g all-natural peanut butter
- 85g monk fruit sweetener
- 160g almond flour
- 1 large egg
- 1 scoop keto collagen powder
- 1g sea salt

1. Preheat the oven to 175°C (155°C fan) and line a baking sheet with parchment paper.
2. In a medium bowl, combine all the ingredients and mix well until combined.
3. Form equal-sized balls using 2 tablespoons of dough and place them on the prepared baking sheet, spacing them about 2 inches apart. Use a fork to press the balls down in a crosshatch pattern.
4. Bake for 12 minutes, then remove from the oven and allow to cool on a wire rack. Store in the refrigerator.

Per Serving

Calories: **44** | Fat: **2.4g** | Protein: **2.4g** | Carbs: **9.3g**

PEANUT BUTTER ICE CREAM

Prep time: **50 minutes** | Cook time: **50 minutes** | Serves **4**

- 125g smooth peanut butter
- 125g erythritol
- 750g half-and-half
- 5g vanilla extract
- A pinch of salt
- 250g raspberries

1. In a bowl, beat the peanut butter and erythritol with a hand mixer until smooth. Gradually whisk in the half-and-half until thoroughly combined. Add the vanilla extract and salt, mixing until incorporated.
2. Transfer the mixture to a loaf tin and freeze for 50 minutes, or until firm. Scoop into glasses and serve topped with raspberries.

Per Serving

Calories: **436** | Fat: **38.5g** | Carbs: **9.5g** | Protein: **13g**

CHAPTER 9

KETO STRAWBERRY ICE CREAM

Prep time: **5 minutes** | Cook time: **3 to 4 hours** | Serves **4**

- 500g full-fat coconut milk
- 125g monk fruit sweetener
- 2 tbsp MCT oil
- 5g vanilla extract
- 200g strawberries, divided

1. In a high-speed blender, combine the coconut milk, monk fruit sweetener, MCT oil, vanilla extract, and half of the strawberries. Blend until smooth.
2. Dice the remaining strawberries and gently fold them into the ice cream mixture.
3. Pour into a freezer-proof glass container and freeze for 3 to 4 hours, or until set.
4. Before serving, allow the ice cream to sit at room temperature for about 10 minutes to soften. Scoop and enjoy.

Per Serving

Calories: **341** | Fat: **35.7g** | Protein: **3g** | Carbs: **13.6g**

OLD-FASHIONED PENUCHE BARS

Prep time: **5 minutes** | Cook time: **45 minutes** | Serves **10**

- 60g butter (½ stick)
- 2 tbsp tahini (sesame paste)
- 125g almond butter
- 5g stevia
- 56g sugar-free baker's chocolate, chopped
- A pinch of salt
- A pinch of grated nutmeg
- 1g ground cinnamon

1. Microwave the butter for 30 to 35 seconds until melted. In a mixing bowl, fold in the tahini, almond butter, stevia, and chopped chocolate until well combined.
2. Sprinkle the mixture with salt, nutmeg, and cinnamon, and whisk to combine. Scrape the mixture into a parchment-lined baking tray.
3. Freeze for 40 minutes, then cut into bars to serve.

Per Serving

Calories: **176** | Fat: **18.3g** | Carbs: **3.2g** | Protein: **1.8g**

NO BAKE ENERGY BITES

Prep time: **5 minutes** | Cook time: **10 minutes** | Serves **10**

- 125g coconut flour
- 125g almond meal
- 65g erythritol
- 2 tbsp milk
- 125g melted peanut butter
- 1g ground cinnamon
- 1g ground star anise
- 5g vanilla paste
- 0.5g coarse sea salt
- 65g sugar-free chocolate chips

1. In a bowl, mix the coconut flour, almond meal, erythritol, milk, melted peanut butter, cinnamon, star anise, vanilla paste, and salt until well combined and smooth.
2. Fold in the chocolate chips until evenly distributed.
3. Spoon the mixture into ice cube trays or moulds.
4. Refrigerate for 1 hour before serving and unmoulding. Enjoy!

Per Serving

Calories: **102** | Fat: **7.8g** | Carbs: **5.8g** | Protein: **2.6g**

APPENDIX 1: MEASUREMENT CONVERSION CHART

MEASUREMENT CONVERSION CHART

VOLUME EQUIVALENTS (DRY)

US STANDARD	METRIC (APPROXIMATE)
1/8 teaspoon	0.5 mL
1/4 teaspoon	1 mL
1/2 teaspoon	2 mL
3/4 teaspoon	4 mL
1 teaspoon	5 mL
1 tablespoon	15 mL
1/4 cup	59 mL
1/2 cup	118 mL
3/4 cup	177 mL
1 cup	235 mL
2 cups	475 mL
3 cups	700 mL
4 cups	1 L

VOLUME EQUIVALENTS (LIQUID)

US STANDARD	US STANDARD (OUNCES)	METRIC (APPROXIMATE)
2 tablespoons	1 fl.oz.	30 mL
1/4 cup	2 fl.oz.	60 mL
1/2 cup	4 fl.oz.	120 mL
1 cup	8 fl.oz.	240 mL
1 1/2 cup	12 fl.oz.	355 mL
2 cups or 1 pint	16 fl.oz.	475 mL
4 cups or 1 quart	32 fl.oz.	1 L
1 gallon	128 fl.oz.	4 L

TEMPERATURES EQUIVALENTS

FAHRENHEIT(F)	CELSIUS(C) (APPROXIMATE)
225 °F	107 °C
250 °F	120 °C
275 °F	135 °C
300 °F	150 °C
325 °F	160 °C
350 °F	180 °C
375 °F	190 °C
400 °F	205 °C
425 °F	220 °C
450 °F	235 °C
475 °F	245 °C
500 °F	260 °C

WEIGHT EQUIVALENTS

US STANDARD	METRIC (APPROXIMATE)
1 ounce	28 g
2 ounces	57 g
5 ounces	142 g
10 ounces	284 g
15 ounces	425 g
16 ounces (1 pound)	455 g
1.5 pounds	680 g
2 pounds	907 g

APPENDIX 2: THE DIRTY DOZEN AND CLEAN FIFTEEN

The Dirty Dozen and Clean Fifteen

The Environmental Working Group (EWG) is a nonprofit, nonpartisan organization dedicated to protecting human health and the environment Its mission is to empower people to live healthier lives in a healthier environment. This organization publishes an annual list of the twelve kinds of produce, in sequence, that have the highest amount of pesticide residue-the Dirty Dozen-as well as a list of the fifteen kinds ofproduce that have the least amount of pesticide residue-the Clean Fifteen.

THE DIRTY DOZEN

- The 2016 Dirty Dozen includes the following produce. These are considered among the year's most important produce to buy organic:

  - Strawberries
  - Apples
  - Nectarines
  - Peaches
  - Celery
  - Grapes
  - Cherries
  - Spinach
  - Tomatoes
  - Bell peppers
  - Cherry tomatoes
  - Cucumbers
  - Kale/collard greens
  - Hot peppers

- The Dirty Dozen list contains two additional itemskale/collard greens and hot peppers-because they tend to contain trace levels of highly hazardous pesticides.

THE CLEAN FIFTEEN

- The least critical to buy organically are the Clean Fifteen list. The following are on the 2016 list:

  - Avocados
  - Corn
  - Pineapples
  - Cabbage
  - Sweet peas
  - Onions
  - Asparagus
  - Mangos
  - Papayas
  - Kiw
  - Eggplant
  - Honeydew
  - Grapefruit
  - Cantaloupe
  - Cauliflower

- Some of the sweet corn sold in the United States are made from genetically engineered (GE) seedstock. Buy organic varieties of these crops to avoid GE produce.

APPENDIX 3: INDEX

A

asparagus 21

avocado 15, 17, 19, 25, 43, 67

B

beef 32, 33, 48, 50, 52

beef bone broth 49

beef chuck 45

beef fat 50

beef stock 45, 49

beef tripe 53

blueberries 17

bone broth 58

broccoli 15, 51, 57, 65, 71

C

cabbage 71

calamari steaks 57

canola oil 35

caraway seeds 70

cauliflower 15, 27, 29, 65, 67, 69

cauliflower rice 51, 59, 69

chia seeds 21, 74

chicken breasts 35, 37, 38, 39, 43

chicken broth 35

chicken drumettes 33, 36

chicken legs 41

chicken mini fillets 39

chicken sausages 21

chicken stock 25, 37, 71

chicken thighs 35, 37, 40

chicken wings 42

chocolate chips 29, 31

chorizo sausage 69

chuck steak 49

cocoa powder 31

coconut cream 29, 81

coconut extract 80

coconut flour 31

coconut milk 17, 19, 65

coconut oil 17, 33, 58

cod fillets 55, 60

coleslaw 52

courgettes 67

cucumber 31, 55

E

erythritol 78, 79, 82

F

fish sauce 39, 42

fish stock 61

flank steak 51

flaxseed 45

flaxseed milk 18

G

goji berries 29

guacamole 59

H

halibut 61

ham 15, 17, 28

hazelnuts 80

hot sauce 35, 47

K

Kalamata olives 31

L

lard 49

Little Gem lettuce leaves 19

M

mayonnaise 17, 27, 55

MCT oil 82

monk fruit sweetener 81

mozzarella 21, 70

mushrooms 13, 19, 72, 53

N

nutmeg 31

O

oregano 15, 31, 33, 37, 41

oyster sauce 35

85

INDEX

P

paprika 35
passata 21, 25
pecans 17
pepperoni 21
pie crust 78
pine nuts 43
pork 52
pork loin 48
pork loin chops 47
pork rinds 33
pork scratchings 21, 39
pork spare ribs 25
prawns 56, 57, 60, 62
prosciutto 32
protein powder 17
pumpkin seeds 74

R

raspberries 81
red curry paste 63

red snapper fillets 63
ricotta 69
rosemary 15
rum 31

S

saffron threads 79, 80
salmon fillets 56, 59, 63
sea scallops 57
shallot 45, 49, 61, 63
Shaoxing rice wine 41
shrimp 58
sirloin steak 47
skirt steak 49, 51
sriracha 52
strawberries 21, 79, 82
sunflower seeds 74

T

tahini 38
tarragon 56

tempeh 66
tilapia fillets 57, 59, 61, 62
trout fillets 61
tuna 24
turkey 33, 36, 40
turkey consommé 36
turkey thighs 35
turkey wings 36

V

vanilla extract 21, 29, 75
vegetable broth 35
vegetable stock 41, 51, 68, 69

W

walnuts 21, 28, 29
white fish fillets 58
Worcestershire sauce 53

X

xylitol 33, 75

Hey there!

Wow, can you believe we've reached the end of this culinary journey together? I'm truly thrilled and filled with joy as I think back on all the recipes we've shared and the flavors we've discovered. This experience, blending a bit of tradition with our own unique twists, has been a journey of love for good food. And knowing you've been out there, giving these dishes a try, has made this adventure incredibly special to me.

Even though we're turning the last page of this book, I hope our conversation about all things delicious doesn't have to end. I cherish your thoughts, your experiments, and yes, even those moments when things didn't go as planned. Every piece of feedback you share is invaluable, helping to enrich this experience for us all.

I'd be so grateful if you could take a moment to share your thoughts with me, be it through a review on Amazon or any other place you feel comfortable expressing yourself online. Whether it's praise, constructive criticism, or even an idea for how we might do things differently in the future, your input is what truly makes this journey meaningful.

This book is a piece of my heart, offered to you with all the love and enthusiasm I have for cooking. But it's your engagement and your words that elevate it to something truly extraordinary.

Thank you from the bottom of my heart for being such an integral part of this culinary adventure. Your openness to trying new things and sharing your experiences has been the greatest gift.

Catch you later,

Betty J. Lawson

Printed in Great Britain
by Amazon